The Long Way Home

"*The Long Way Home* is a heartfelt reminder that each of us experiences a unique and deeply personal journey with our Heavenly Father. Jeff's relatable story of faith encourages us that in our quiet acts of trust, receptivity, and pursuit, we discover the depth of God's love. For anyone with a loved one who has drifted away, Jeff's journey offers hope and reassurance that it's never too late to take the first step back home."

—JENNIFER MURPHY, Founder, Inspire & Transform Consulting

"Reading Jeff's story is like looking through a window into someone's soul and seeing the immense satisfaction that comes from pursuing a deeper relationship with Christ and the Catholic Church. Use this book as a roadmap to return to—or discover for the first time—the fullness of faith offered to those willing to ask, seek, and knock on the door."

—BETSY ORR, Founder, Heritage, Georgia

"There is no story more compelling than that of someone finding their way back home—especially when, over time, they didn't even realize they were lost. *The Long Way Home* is part heartfelt testimonial, part practical guide: an honest, real-life account of a wanderer rediscovering his spiritual roots. It's a journey that will both inspire and equip you to begin your own."

—LON ROBERTS, author's friend and professional colleague

"In *The Long Way Home* Jeff Lukich shares his story of coming back to his faith and the Lord's Church in a winsome, vulnerable, and attractive manner. This allows Jeff to gently lead and guide any reader considering a return to their Catholic faith. Jeff has offered pastors and church leaders a great tool to accompany Catholics as they consider returning home to the Lord's church."

—MARK WHITE, Pastor, St. Joseph's Catholic Church, Washington, Georgia

The Long Way Home

A Catholic Return to Faith—How I Found My Way Home, and How You Can Too

JEFF LUKICH

RESOURCE *Publications* • Eugene, Oregon

THE LONG WAY HOME
A Catholic Return to Faith—How I Found My Way Home, and How You Can Too

Copyright © 2025 Jeff Lukich. All rights reserved. Except for brief quotations in critical publications or reviews, no part of this book may be reproduced in any manner without prior written permission from the publisher. Write: Permissions, Wipf and Stock Publishers, 199 W. 8th Ave., Suite 3, Eugene, OR 97401.

Resource Publications
An Imprint of Wipf and Stock Publishers
199 W. 8th Ave., Suite 3
Eugene, OR 97401

www.wipfandstock.com

PAPERBACK ISBN: 979-8-3852-5325-8
HARDCOVER ISBN: 979-8-3852-5326-5
EBOOK ISBN: 979-8-3852-5327-2
VERSION NUMBER 11/05/25

Scripture quotations are from the *Revised Standard Version, Second Catholic Edition* (RSV-2CE), copyright © 1965, 1966 by the Division of Christian Education of the National Council of the Churches of Christ in the United States of America. Used by permission. All rights reserved worldwide.

*For every Catholic who has drifted away.
May God's grace and love guide you back home.*

*In the name of the Father,
and of the Son,
and of the Holy Spirit.
Amen.*

Contents

Acknowledgments | ix
Introduction | xi

1. The Long Way Home—A Personal Journey | 1
2. Why People Leave—And Why There's Always Hope | 16
3. Taking the First Step—The Courage to Reach Out | 29
4. Reconciliation—Embracing a Fresh Start | 43
5. Finding Your Place in the Parish—A Time of Renewal | 58
6. Living Out Your Faith—Strengthening Yourself and Reaching Others | 74
7. Keeping the Faith—A Lifelong Pilgrimage | 90
8. When the People You Love Are Far From Faith | 103
9. Welcome Home—The Joy of Embracing God's Love | 112

Epilogue | 120
Appendix—Suggested Readings, Online Resources, and Prayers | 123
Bibliography | 127

Acknowledgments

I AM DEEPLY GRATEFUL to my wife, Mary Beth, whose love, encouragement, and patience carried me through the long hours of writing. Her steady support made this book possible: she prayed for me, gave me the space and time I needed to work, and believed in this project even when I doubted myself.

To my close friends, along with a few parish members who have been especially supportive, thank you for your support and prayers. Your encouragement often came in small ways, simply asking, "How's the book going?" On the surface, it may have seemed like a casual question, but to me it meant that you were thinking about me. Those moments gave me opportunities to talk more about the story and what matters most to me, and in a way, to share the faith that inspired it.

I especially want to thank Fr. Mark White of my parish, Saint Joseph's Catholic Church, who has been present from the very beginning of my return. When I first met with him, my path could have gone either way, but his patience, understanding, and knowledge made my return easier. He is never a barrier to those seeking the Church, but welcomes all with guidance and support. I believe my journey home could not have unfolded as it did without him.

My thanks also to Wipf and Stock Publishers for believing in this story and giving it the chance to reach others. I am grateful to my editor, as well as the production, design, and marketing teams at Wipf and Stock, whose careful work brought this manuscript into its final form.

Acknowledgments

I am thankful for a few trusted friends who read portions of the manuscript along the way or served as beta readers, offering feedback that helped strengthen the final work. I am also grateful to those who generously endorsed this book; your encouragement and willingness to stand with me on this project gave me confidence when I needed it most.

I also want to thank, in a special way, all those Catholics who have drifted from the Church. Although I do not know each of you personally, you were very much in my heart as I wrote these pages. Your struggles, questions, and hopes inspired me, and I continue to pray for you often.

In writing this book, I am grateful to be living in a time when writers have access to digital tools, including some powered by AI. For me, they served as practical aids in organization, research, and copyediting. They also became a sounding board, helping me clarify ideas and giving me more space to focus on the story I wanted to tell and the people I hoped to reach. These tools only provided editorial and organizational support; the message and final words are my own. Guided by the Church's recent reflection, *Antiqua et Nova: Note on the Relationship Between Artificial Intelligence and Human Intelligence*, I regard AI simply as a tool at the service of human creativity.

Above all, I give thanks to God, who led me home and gave me the grace to share this story. I am grateful every day that He brought me back into the Catholic Church. Being part of her life again—the beauty of the Mass, the sacraments, and the community—has become one of the greatest joys of my life. All the glory goes to Him.

Introduction

I NEVER SET OUT to write this book. I was simply trying to find my way home. After forty years away from my Catholic faith, years spent searching, questioning, and even running from what I knew to be true, I found myself sitting beside my wife in a pew on Christmas Eve 2022. It was my first Mass since 1987. I was overcome by a peace I hadn't felt in decades. But even then, I still had doubts and couldn't fully understand what I was feeling. All I knew was that God was calling me, and this felt like home. There were no dramatic signs or flashes of light from heaven, just a quiet, unmistakable sense that I was exactly where I belonged.

This book is the story of that return. Not just mine, but the return that's possible for anyone who's ever felt far from the Church, from God, or their faith. I don't share these pages as an expert, but as someone who has walked the long road back and learned what makes the first steps possible and the next steps lasting. It isn't heavy with theology, and it's not about stirring up guilt. It's an honest invitation to come home, no matter how long you've been away or how far you feel right now. By the final page, I hope you'll be well on your way, with the encouragement and strength to remain close to the faith that has always been yours.

WHO THIS BOOK IS FOR

This book is for the Catholic who hasn't been to Mass in years and wonders if they'd even be welcomed back. It's for the person who

Introduction

believes in God but isn't sure how—or if—the Church still fits into their life. It's also for the cradle Catholic who slowly drifted away, the person curious about what the Catholic faith can offer their life today, and the parent who raised children in another tradition but now feels a pull to return. It's for those who've been hurt or disappointed by the Church yet can't quite shake the sense that something meaningful is missing.

It's also for the person who isn't sure where to begin, the one who feels like too much time has passed, and the one who's taken a first step back but isn't sure how to make it last. Wherever you find yourself, whether hesitant, curious, halfway home, or already walking through the door, these pages are meant to meet you there.

You won't find judgment here. Instead, you'll find honesty, encouragement, and companionship for the road ahead. You won't find a rulebook or a checklist here. What you will find is space to wrestle with questions, rediscover what drew you to faith, and return without fear or pressure. We'll take things one step at a time, beginning right where you are and moving toward a faith that feels both familiar and new.

WHAT IT FEELS LIKE TO BE AWAY

Stepping away from the Church doesn't always look like rebellion. For me, it felt more like an emptiness, something I couldn't explain. Life carried me along: family, work, even occasional worship in other places, but I knew deep down that something was missing. In the silence, I simply felt my heart being pulled.

You may feel ashamed, disconnected, or uncertain about what you truly believe. For me, the most significant barrier was fear. Fear that I wouldn't know what to do, that I'd forgotten the prayers, that after so many years, I might not be accepted back. Those worries kept me from answering God's call for a long time. I didn't know if coming back was even an option. All I knew was that I felt lost.

I wrote this book from that "in-between" space—the place where you're searching, hoping, and maybe even afraid to take the

Introduction

first step. If that's where you are today, know this—there is a way *home*, and it's more familiar than you might think.

As I write this, we are in the Jubilee Holy Year of 2025, marking the 2,025th anniversary of the Incarnation of our Lord, a deeply meaningful event in the life of the Church. Pope Francis first called us to embrace this year as a time of renewal, reconciliation, and pilgrimage, inviting us to be "Pilgrims of Hope." Pope Leo XIV has since carried that call forward. For me, being a pilgrim of hope means trusting that every step toward God matters. It means believing that home isn't something you have to earn, because it's always been yours. If you've felt even a quiet pull to return, I believe that's no accident. God may be inviting you to begin now, not later. My prayer is that these pages will be a companion on your own pilgrimage, offering comfort, clarity, and hope.

WHAT YOU'LL FIND IN THESE PAGES

The journey you're about to read begins with the early feelings of return: the memories, questions, and nudges that can draw us back to God. From there, we'll move into the first practical steps of returning to the Church, which include facing fears, reconnecting with prayer, and easing back into the rhythm of the sacraments.

We'll explore what it's like to take your place again in a parish community, rebuild a personal relationship with God, and live your faith in ways that are both joyful and sustainable. And finally, we'll look ahead to what it means to keep the faith for a lifetime, staying rooted in Christ through seasons of change, doubt, and growth. Whether you're just beginning to think about returning or you've already begun, I hope these chapters will give you both the courage to start and the strength to stay.

Your home is still there. It's waiting for you. Even now, God is reaching out to welcome you back.

With hope,
Jeff Lukich, 2025

1

The Long Way Home
A Personal Journey

RETURNING TO MY CHILDHOOD CHURCH

THE WEEK AFTER CHRISTMAS 2024, I made my way back to St. Mary's Catholic Church, the small church in the South Carolina low country where I grew up. Two years after returning to the Catholic Church, I found myself sitting in a pew at St. Mary's, the same church where my faith had begun. I didn't expect it to feel so meaningful, but it did. As I knelt there, I realized something important—God had been guiding me home long before I even knew I needed to return.

This trip wasn't spontaneous. I had planned it.

My family had spent the week between Christmas and New Year's on the South Carolina coast, not far from Charleston. It should have been a relaxing trip, but in reality, it had been a long, noisy, chaotic week. The kind of week that reminded me how much I love my family, but also how much I sometimes needed time alone.

So, I had planned a quick overnight trip back home to Georgia, telling everyone I needed to check on the house, which was true. But the bigger truth was that I had planned my drive home so I could attend Mass on Sunday morning at St. Mary's. I needed this. I needed to come back.

The rain was coming down hard as I pulled up to the front of St. Mary's. I sat in my truck for a moment, watching the water streak down the windshield, blurring the edges of the blue-gray building in front of me. It looked just as it always had. The windows on either side of the church stood out, just as they had when I was a boy. I could still picture the scene from years ago—the families from the parish stepping out into the sunlight after Mass, standing in small circles, talking, catching up, my mother among them. My friends and I were waiting impatiently for the adults to finish so we could leave.

And now, I was back. It had been over forty years.

I stepped out of the truck and pulled my jacket tighter against the cold rain. As I approached the church and placed my hand on the door, I paused, then pushed it open. It was the smell that hit me first, just as it had when I was a child. A mix of old wood, incense, and something else, something familiar, something unchanged.

I took a few slow steps inside, letting my eyes adjust to the lighting. A few people were already seated, scattered in the pews. Would I recognize anyone after all this time? I stood near the back, hesitating for a moment.

Where do I sit? The answer came without thinking. The same place I always sat as a child.

I made my way up the aisle and slid into a pew near the end, settling into a spot where, for years, I had sat beside my mom and brothers. The wooden pew creaked a bit as I knelt to pray. I clasped my hands together and lowered my head, but instead of words, all I felt was a wave of emotion.

Fifteen years. That's how long it had been since my mother passed. And the truth was, we weren't close when she died. There were things left unsaid and never made right between us. But one thing was certain—no matter our differences, the greatest gift she ever gave me was bringing me into the Church. Even when I drifted away, that foundation was always there, waiting for me to return.

Why was it hitting me now?

Maybe it was sitting here, in this very pew, where she had once knelt in prayer. Or perhaps it was just the weight of time—realizing how much had changed, how much I had changed. I wasn't the same person I was two years ago.

I closed my eyes and whispered a prayer. For her. For my family. For peace. For the things I couldn't go back and fix.

Mass wouldn't start for a while, so I sat back and took in the surroundings. Though the church had been updated over the years, it still somehow looked the same. The crucifix above the altar was the same one I had stared at as a boy. The statues of Mary and Joseph remained on either side of the sanctuary, just as they always had. Despite the changes, nothing truly felt different. It was as if I had never left.

A man sat alone in the back of the church. I walked over and asked if he knew where the bathroom was. He shook his head and chuckled. "I'm visiting too," he said.

Up near the ambo, an altar server was setting up the Missal for Mass. He was flipping pages back and forth, muttering under his breath, visibly frustrated. "Where are the readings?" he mumbled, shaking his head. He flipped through the book again, sighed, and tried another section.

As an altar server at my parish back in Georgia, I almost offered to help for a moment. But I stayed in my pew, watching. There was something oddly familiar about the scene. An ordinary moment, yet it reminded me just how much I had missed being in a church like this.

Still needing to find the restroom, I walked up to him and asked where it was. He glanced up from the Missal and pointed toward a side door. "Through there," he said, still distracted and irritated at this point.

I followed his direction and stepped through the accordion-style door, expecting to find a small hallway or utility room on the other side. Instead, I found myself in a small classroom. I stopped. The room was small and simple—just a few chairs, a whiteboard, and some religious posters tacked onto the walls. And then it hit me. This was the same classroom where I had attended Catechism before my confirmation in 1977.

It had changed over the years, updated with different furniture, yet I could still picture myself sitting there as a child, listening to lessons on the sacraments and memorizing prayers. I had learned so much about being Catholic in this room. And now, decades later, I had returned. Not just to the Church, but to the exact place where my Catholic foundation had been laid.

The moment was heavy.

This may be why I had planned this trip. Maybe this was why I had felt such a strong pull to come back to this church, on this day, in this moment.

I closed my eyes for a second and let it settle in. This was no accident.

After sitting back in the pew, another memory surfaced. One I hadn't thought about in years.

When we first moved to town, after my mom left my dad, our house was just two blocks from St. Mary's. Close enough that my older brother and I could walk to Mass alone on Sundays. And for a while, we did.

My mom didn't come with us at first. I don't know why. Maybe it was because she was separated from my dad. Maybe the divorce was still in process, and she was trying to sort things out with the Church before coming back. Maybe she felt embarrassed. Or maybe, in her own way, she was still wrestling with what it all meant—for her, and for us.

That was the thing about my mother. She was religious, but she also had a way of making things personal. Looking back, I think her struggles with faith may have had more to do with her personal circumstances than with anything God had done.

But whatever the reason, she eventually started attending Mass with us again. It became part of our Sundays, something we shared as a family. Something normal.

Now, decades later, I was the one returning alone.

By the time Mass began, a few more people had arrived, but the parish was still small, just as I remembered. I overheard the priest chatting with a few parishioners and realized he hadn't been there in a while. It made sense, as parishes like this were often served by rotating priests from a larger church in a nearby town.

The liturgy was the same as it always was. That's the beauty of Catholicism: no matter where you go or how long you've been away, the Mass is constant. It is a true comfort.

And then came the Eucharist.

Walking up the aisle, I felt something I hadn't felt in a long time. A deep, overwhelming feeling of gratitude. Thanking God again for calling me back.

Two years after my return to my Catholic faith, if someone asks me the number one reason why I am Catholic? It is the truth, gift, and sacrifice of the Eucharist. Receiving the Eucharist in the very same church where I received my first Holy Communion was a spiritually emotional experience for me. As I walked back to my pew, I knew without a doubt—God had called me home.

Sitting in that pew, I realized something important—I had left the Catholic Church, but I had never truly walked away from God. This moment, returning to where it all began, was proof that God had been guiding me all along.

Being in that pew again brought me back to the beginning. I didn't leave the Church overnight; it was a slow process, shaped by how I was raised in the faith. To really explain my return, I have to tell you about those early years and what being Catholic meant to me then.

GROWING UP CATHOLIC

My mom left my dad in 1973. At the time, she had two boys, my older brother and me, and she was pregnant with my younger brother. I won't use their names here, but their presence is part of this story. Looking back now, as a 58-year-old, I can't imagine how hard it must have been for my mom to raise three boys alone. Being a single mother is never easy, but in the Catholic Church of the 1970s, I imagine it came with added weight. Divorce wasn't talked about much, and it carried a quiet stigma.

From early on, her parenting was structured and full of high expectations, sometimes more rigid than I could understand at the time. As a child, I often experienced her rules and the Church's teachings as one and the same. I couldn't always tell where her rules stopped and the Church's began. But looking back, I can see how much she cared about our spiritual well-being, especially when we were younger and more active in the Church. That part of her—the desire to keep us grounded in faith—has stayed with me.

Even with that strictness, I felt a secret pride in being Catholic.

Being Catholic felt special to me as a child, though it's hard to describe exactly why. There weren't many Catholics in my small southern town. I didn't fully understand the sacraments, but I knew they mattered. I'm not sure I would've even called it "faith" at that age, but I knew I belonged to something meaningful.

Still, being Catholic also felt heavy at times. The message I picked up, whether intended or not, was that we were sinners, *always* falling short. While that may be true, I didn't get that same feeling when I occasionally attended Protestant churches with friends. Those services felt lighter somehow.

My mother worked hard, but we still grew up poor. As a kid, I sometimes felt like the Church's message to families like ours was simply to accept our circumstances. I now understand that the heart of that message was to trust in God, but at the time, it felt more like resignation than hope.

Our local parish in that small South Carolina town was a good place. I loved that church. And for much of my childhood, we had a wonderful priest: kind, approachable, the type of man who lived his faith out loud. I won't use his name, but I remember him well. He spent his time helping others, repairing homes, patching roofs, fixing what he could.

The summer before I started high school, he let me tag along on some of his work projects. That summer, I learned how to shingle a roof, but I also learned much more. He worked harder than I ever expected a priest would, and it was clear this was a mission for him, not just a side task. He was patient with me as I tried to learn the basics of roofing, carpentry, and small repairs. What stayed with me was the way he lived out service: showing up, doing the work well, and caring for people in practical ways. At the time, I didn't think of it as faith in action, but looking back, it planted a seed that later shaped how I now serve in my parish. In many ways, he gave me an example of living faith that I hadn't seen at home.

The parish community helped us too. I remember the priest showing up with a check to help cover the power bill or help us through a tough stretch. I sometimes wondered if my mother leaned too heavily on that generosity, but the truth is, we needed it. And the Church provided. God provided.

Looking back, I see how much the Church provided for us, not just materially, but spiritually. Prayer became my quiet way of staying connected to that faith.

Prayer has always been a part of my life, even as a child. My mom didn't emphasize it much, but I remember praying at night. Sometimes for things I wanted, but often for people. I prayed for my dad, who was still in Charleston. I prayed for my family. Even then, I felt an inward pull toward God.

We went to Mass nearly every Sunday. I've always valued routine; as a child, that rhythm brought me comfort, especially when life felt uncertain. When we missed, I felt guilty.

By high school, I had started skipping Mass for no good reason. I had a conversation with our priest about it once. He made it clear that Mass wasn't optional. I understand now that Sundays are days of obligation. But at the time, it just felt like one more rule. That sense that faith was mostly about rules and guilt was one of the reasons I began to drift during my teen years.

By the time I was in high school, my older brother had already left for college. It was just my younger brother and me at home. We still went to church, but less and less. And I noticed my mom slowly drifting too. There was an unhappiness building in her that I didn't fully understand at the time. It surprised me, given how strong her Catholic upbringing had been. She had grown up in southwestern Pennsylvania, in a devout Catholic family. Maybe the distance from her siblings, who still lived up north, made it harder. Or faith felt less connected without her family and the people she'd grown up with.

As the years went on, my brothers' paths with faith moved in different directions from mine. It reminded me that even within the same family, faith is deeply personal.

I left for college in the fall of 1984. I was ready. I attended Spartanburg Methodist College in the upstate of South Carolina, the same school my older brother had attended. It was a small, liberal arts Methodist college. Even though it wasn't Catholic, it was faith-based, and I still felt connected to God, just without the heaviness I had felt in the Catholic Church. I met other Christians and occasionally attended chapel on campus. But I didn't go often.

After my sophomore year, I transferred to Presbyterian College, also in South Carolina, and completed my degree in political science and history.

By then, I had stopped attending church altogether, unless I went with my girlfriend's family in Georgia. At the end of my freshman year, my mom had moved to a small town in Georgia, where I still live today. By then, my mom had stopped attending Mass altogether. Her connection to her faith seemed to have faded entirely.

Those childhood years gave me a foundation, but as I grew older, the weight of rules and expectations began to overshadow the sense of belonging. By the time I left for college, that tension had pulled me further away. Walking out of the Church at eighteen felt easy enough, but letting go of God was something I couldn't do.

That's one of my deepest regrets. I spent forty years without the sacraments. Forty years without the Eucharist, which is now the lifeblood of my faith.

DRIFTING AWAY—BUT NEVER FROM GOD

By the time I graduated from college in 1989, I had entirely drifted from the Catholic faith. And as I stepped into adult life, marriage, work, and raising a family, that drift gradually widened over time. It wasn't a rebellion. I wasn't angry at the Church. I simply let go of organized religion without much thought. Like many people, I thought I could make it on my own.

I married Mary Beth that fall, just a few months after graduating. She had grown up in a small country church just outside of Washington, Georgia, where we'd eventually settle down ourselves. She knew very little about the Catholic faith. We were married in the Methodist Church, where we also raised our children. That became the new rhythm of our spiritual life, shaped mainly by her example and steady commitment to Christianity.

In the early years of our marriage, I attended church sporadically, mostly on holidays or when we visited her parents, who still lived in Washington. We lived in nearby Augusta early in our marriage, so it was easy to stay connected initially, but over time, my attendance waned even further. Not intentionally. Just slowly.

I didn't stop believing in God. In fact, I often felt more spiritual than those around me, including my family.

I adopted a "me and Jesus" mindset, thinking that personal belief and private connection were enough. I never stopped feeling that God was present in my life, but I was wrong in thinking that was all I needed. I understand that now.

Looking back, one of my deepest regrets is that I wasn't a better spiritual leader in my home, especially for my children. I should have talked more about my faith—a lot more.

My wife carried that weight, ensuring our kids were involved in church and surrounded by a spiritual community.

For that, I'm grateful.

Even as my faith life faded into the background, endurance sports took its place. What began as a personal challenge soon became a defining part of who I was. Running, then later swimming and cycling, began to shape not only how I spent my time, but how I managed stress, set goals, and even measured success. It gave me structure, community, and purpose, things I didn't realize I was missing spiritually. Competing in long-distance races became a regular part of my life, and I poured myself into the training with the kind of discipline I now apply to my faith.

Throughout my 30s and 40s, life was full. I was building a career in public child welfare, working long hours in a high-stress field. I was also raising kids, training for races, and traveling to compete in endurance events, including marathons, triathlons, and Ironman races, which required 12 to 17 hours of training each week. I used to say my church was out on my bike. That was how I explained away skipping Sunday services. I'd head out early, ride for hours, and tell myself it was just a different kind of worship. And sure, it cleared my head. It gave me space to think. But I wasn't praying out there. I wasn't seeking God. I was just trying to be my own bishop. My own pope. Following my own rules. Answering only to myself.

Even then, I felt a strong connection to God. But it wasn't rooted. I didn't have a consistent prayer life. I wasn't reading scripture. There was no spiritual direction, no sacraments.

Just belief—quiet, persistent, but largely unformed.

As I climbed into leadership roles at work, my stress increased. I eventually oversaw daily operations in one of the largest state agencies in Georgia. The responsibility was intense, especially during the final five years of my career. The hours got longer, and my ability to manage anything outside of work and training began to wear thin. Toward the end, it was taking a toll on me: mentally, physically, and spiritually.

Still, I didn't know what was missing. I just couldn't see it yet. I had always felt like I was searching for something, but I couldn't name it. I certainly didn't think it was the Catholic Church. I was still carrying some bitterness I hadn't yet fully unpacked. But the truth is, I didn't realize how far I had drifted until I began to feel something pulling me back.

For years, life kept moving—marriage, raising kids, long hours at work, and the steady rhythm of training and racing. Faith was in the background, but it wasn't my anchor. Looking back, I can see how empty that left me, even if I didn't admit it at the time. That gap set the stage for what came next: the turning point that finally brought me home.

THE TURNING POINT

Looking back, I see now that God had been calling me home in subtle ways long before I recognized it. The final five years of my career were some of the hardest. I served as Chief of Staff with the Georgia Division of Family and Children Services in the high-risk environment of public child welfare. At the same time, I was racing frequently (two to four big events each year), often including one or two full Ironman races. I competed across the U.S. and Canada, working more than 50 hours a week and training six days a week. My job had me traveling all over the state, and while I was mostly energized during this season of life, I couldn't shake the feeling that I was lost. I continued to pray, but mostly for myself, and not in a way that involved *listening to God*. I rarely went to church with my family. During this time, I began visiting the *Catholics Come Home* website on my own. I read and reflected, but I wasn't sure this was the direction God was calling me.

I didn't feel ready.

I retired in 2018 after 30 years with the State of Georgia, though I stayed active in consulting work until 2023. I was only 51, but given the circumstances within our division and the fact that our two-term governor was leaving office, it felt like the right time. That decision came with an overwhelming sense of peace. I genuinely believe it was one of the moments God spoke clearly to me. For the first time in decades, I had room to breathe and space to reflect. I began thinking more deeply about faith. Still, I wasn't certain whether I was being called back to the Catholic Church or simply being called out of sin. Maybe both.

For decades, I had lived in a kind of spiritual "neutral." I believed in God. I prayed, but not deeply or consistently. I knew something was missing, but I kept chasing all the wrong things. Even when I started reading on the *Catholics Come Home* website, I struggled with uncertainty, lack of confidence, and fear. Would I feel out of place again, like I had in Protestant churches over the years? Would I be welcomed? Could I really go back after being away for so long?

The real turning point came on Christmas Eve 2022. Mary Beth and I had been watching *It's a Wonderful Life*, as we often did during the holidays. That day, I felt a deep pull, and I told her, "I need to go to Mass tonight." I hadn't been to a Catholic Mass since 1987.

This was a big step.

We found St. Joseph's, the local Catholic church in Washington, and saw that there was a 7:00 PM Christmas Eve Mass. I found out later that this was unusual for the parish in recent years, as many often attended a nearby historical Catholic church for Christmas Eve.

Walking into the church that night, I was nervous. But I was also immediately struck by how much this parish resembled St. Mary's, the church where I grew up in South Carolina. The crucifix. The statues of Mary and Joseph. Even the windows. It felt familiar.

We sat down, and I looked around, feeling waves of recognition and memory. When the Mass began, everything came flooding back. Within ten minutes, I realized—this is what I had been missing all along. The prayers. The ritual. The reverence. The Eucharist. The distinct way that Catholics worship. I couldn't take the Eucharist that night, but I was overcome with emotion during that part of the liturgy. I felt God's presence in a way I hadn't felt in years. It was personal. It was sacred.

I was home.

After the holidays, I found the priest's email address on the parish website and reached out. He responded quickly, and we set up a meeting for mid-January 2023. In the meantime, Mary Beth and I continued attending Sunday Mass. The people at St. Joseph's were so welcoming, which made a big difference for me. I'm an introvert, and being social at church has never come naturally. But this felt different.

The priest and I talked for over 90 minutes. After being away for 40 years, I had a lot of questions: about confession, views on women's role in the Church, same-sex couples, and more. I still tended to think in political terms, but he kindly helped me reframe my thinking. He reminded me that when we separate faith from politics, we begin to see more clearly the truth of God's plan for us through the Church. I was ready to make my first confession, but he encouraged me to slow down and to take more time for reflection. Then he asked about my marriage. I told him that Mary Beth and I had been married in the Methodist Church 33 years earlier. He explained what I initially understood as "having our marriage blessed" in the Church. But "convalidation", a term I had never heard before, turned out to be much more than that.

Convalidation in the Catholic Church is more than a blessing; it's a sacramental act that affirms the couple's vows within the Church's understanding of marriage. It was also a necessary step for me to return in full communion with the Church. It was difficult when I came home and tried to explain this to Mary Beth. I left the meeting full of excitement and energy, but I stumbled when it came to explaining what the Church was asking. At first, it sounded like I was saying our marriage hadn't been valid for all those years. That was painful for Mary Beth to hear. At the beginning of this journey, I only asked her to attend Mass with me. I never expected her to convert. That decision came later, and it was hers alone, guided by the Holy Spirit.

However, after a conversation with the priest and a clearer explanation of what convalidation really meant, she understood. We had shared 33 years of marriage, with a love and life together that were genuine and lasting. Still, the Church offered us something deeper: the grace of rooting our vows in the sacramental life.

Through convalidation, we didn't erase our marriage. We completed it.

A few weeks later, we had a small private ceremony with two parish witnesses, a couple we had known casually over the years at St. Joseph's. Mary Beth and I thought this would be just an administrative step, something required for me to fully return to the Church and for her to begin the path toward conversion. But it was more than that. We exchanged vows again. It was the complete sacrament of marriage. It was meaningful and intimate. And we now celebrate that day, March 16, 2023, as our Catholic marriage anniversary.

Those first few months back in the Church were full of joy and peace. I didn't just return. I pursued my faith with a depth I had never experienced. For the first time in my adult life, I prayed with scripture. The sacraments became real and personal. I joined what was then called RCIA, the Rite of Christian Initiation of Adults, with Mary Beth. Today, it's known as OCIA, but the purpose remains the same: to help adults prepare to enter the Church. I wasn't just there to relearn Catholic teaching. I was there to walk with her, as her sponsor. Her decision to become Catholic was never something I asked for, but it remains one of the greatest gifts of this journey. I watched as she wrestled with new teachings and asked her own questions—not out of obligation, but with genuine curiosity. Seeing her discover the beauty of the sacraments for herself deepened my own faith. Watching her take that step with such openness and courage has left me grateful in ways I didn't expect.

Alongside RCIA, I joined an adult Bible study for the first time. And then, within six months of returning, I felt called to serve at the altar. I was trained as an altar server and learned how to assist in the sacristy. Serving alongside our priest and deacon is one of the greatest joys of my life, not just because it allows me to contribute to my parish, but because I feel drawn closer to the Eucharist. To this day, I still get emotional during that part of the Mass.

In early Lent of 2023, I made my first confession in 40 years. It was profound. Emotional. A weight had been lifted. Next to the Eucharist, the gift of Reconciliation is one of the reasons I'm Catholic. That first confession marked a turning point. The old version of me was gone. I knew I was no longer the same. I saw myself as a son of God. Knowing how deeply Jesus loves me and that He forgives me no matter what still overwhelms me.

Today, nearly three years later, I'm fully involved in our parish. Mary Beth came into the Church in July 2023. I serve at the altar on Sundays, sit on the church council, and volunteer when I can. The friendships I've formed at St. Joseph's have been vital to this journey. I'll talk more about that in a later chapter, but I can say this now: I didn't just come back to Church. I came back to life.

Coming home to the Church changed everything. But the truth is, I'm not the only one who left, and I'm not the only one who's come back. In the next chapter, we'll look at why people leave the Catholic Church, how so many—like me—find their way back, and why others never do.

2

Why People Leave
And Why There's Always Hope

BEFORE WE CAN TALK about the journey back, we need to understand why so many people step away. For some, it's a struggle with Church teachings. For others, it's a gradual drifting away, or a life event that disrupts their connection to faith.

I've learned, both through my research and personal experience, that the reasons people leave are often complex, layered, emotional, and rarely the result of a single moment or decision. In this chapter, I want to explore those reasons with compassion and without judgment. The goal isn't to analyze or assign blame. It's to open the door to healing, restoration, and the possibility of return.

One thing that stands out in the data is how early this disconnection often begins. Nearly half of former Catholics leave before the age of 18, and about three in ten step away during young adulthood, between 18 and 23. I was in that latter group, drifting away when I left for college. These numbers reinforce just how important solid faith formation is during adolescence and young adulthood, both at home and within the Church. Those years are about planting seeds that may not bear fruit until much later.

STRUGGLES WITH CHURCH TEACHINGS OR EXPERIENCE

It's no surprise that one of the most common reasons people leave the Church is because they struggle with its teachings or have had a negative experience with a church leader, parish culture, or Catholic education. Sometimes it's a disagreement over doctrine, such as the Church's position on abortion, contraception, or the authority of the Pope. Other times, it's a painful experience with a priest or teacher. In some cases, people lose belief in the fundamentals of the faith, like Christ's real presence in the Eucharist. For others, the difficulty lies in teachings on sexuality, divorce, the role of women in the Church, or moral issues they find hard to reconcile.

This kind of struggle isn't rare. It's actually part of the journey for many Catholics, even for those who stay. It was certainly part of mine. When I returned to the Church, I realized that some of the issues I thought I disagreed with were really things I hadn't fully understood. That shift in mindset made a big difference for me. Instead of framing my questions as opposition, I began to see them as invitations to learn more, reflect more deeply, and have honest conversations with my priest when I needed clarity.

Some Church teachings are challenging, and some are deeply personal. When they touch our lives directly, the emotional weight can make it hard to stay. But I've come to believe that wrestling with faith is not a sign of rejection. It's often a sign of spiritual depth. We're not called to blind agreement but to seek, ask, and grow in our relationship with Christ.

If you find yourself in that space—uncertain, questioning, maybe even angry—I encourage you to be patient with yourself. Give yourself room to grow. Ask the hard questions. Talk to someone you trust. But most of all, pray. Scripture, quiet reflection, and honest conversation with God can open the heart in ways no argument or article ever could. For me, the clearest insights haven't come from someone giving me the correct answer; they've come in moments of prayer, when I was finally ready to listen. One prayer I've returned to again and again is: *Lord, help me to see what*

I cannot yet see. And every day, I also pray: *Jesus, please help me see others and this world through your love-filled eyes.*

GRADUAL DISCONNECTION

For many, the drift from the Church isn't rooted in disagreement or crisis. It's quieter than that. It starts slowly—missing Mass here and there, falling out of regular prayer, becoming less involved at the parish. Life gets busy. Demands increase. Careers, parenting, and daily pressures take priority. And over time, without even noticing, that once-familiar sense of belonging begins to fade.

That's how it happened, in part, for me. There was no big decision to leave; it was just a slow, steady loosening of the connection. One season in life bled into the next, and faith gradually moved to the background. I still believed in God, but the practices that once grounded me weren't part of my life anymore.

Sometimes, the questioning or disconnection surfaces during particular life events: a cross-country move, the death of a loved one, a divorce, or even a period of emotional stress. In those moments, we may not reject faith outright, but we stop reaching for it. The reasons vary, but the pattern is *gradual*, familiar, and more common than many of us realize. Have you ever looked back and realized just how far you'd drifted from the habits that once anchored your faith?

LIFE TRANSITIONS AND DISRUPTIONS

Not all spiritual disconnection happens slowly. Sometimes, it's sudden. A move, an illness, a job change, or other life events can shake the routine of our lives and displace our connection to faith almost overnight. In these moments, the disruption comes from the outside. And if we're not careful, it can last much longer than we intended. These may be expected, like starting a new job or becoming a parent, or they may catch us off guard, like a sudden illness or a family crisis.

Why People Leave

One survey I reviewed showed that nearly 20 percent of people who left the Church cited moving away from their home parish as the primary reason. That would include those who left for college, as I did. Another 17 percent said that moving away from family was a turning point in their spiritual disconnection. A change in geography often brings a change in our life structure. As we adjust to new routines and responsibilities, faith can easily slip out of view.

In my case, leaving home for college marked the beginning of my departure from the Church. But the season that pulled me farthest from spiritual grounding was much later, during the final stretch of my career. The demands of my work life, especially in those last five years, became all-consuming. My faith didn't disappear, but it faded into the background. And yet, in those years, something new began to stir in me. I felt a growing pull back toward God and, eventually, to His Church.

Transitions can create distance from faith—that part is familiar to many of us. Disruptions in life do more than inconvenience us. They can gently nudge us back to what matters most. They can open up space to hear God again and remind us that faith isn't just habit or routine, but a relationship with Christ.

SPIRITUAL NEEDS NOT BEING MET

One consistent theme that emerged as I researched for this chapter was that many former Catholics left the Church because they felt their *spiritual needs weren't being met*. This phrase may sound vague at first, but when you look more closely, it often points to something deeply personal. It's not necessarily about disagreeing with doctrine; it's about feeling disconnected from God, uninspired by worship, or spiritually unfulfilled within parish life.

According to the Pew Research Center's *Faith in Flux: Changes in Religious Affiliation in the U.S.* survey (2009), 71 percent of former Catholics who became Protestant said their spiritual needs weren't being met, and named it as the primary reason they left. That included both those who became unaffiliated and those who joined Protestant communities. For some, that disconnection grew gradually, like other patterns we've already explored in this chapter. But for many, it reached a point where the Church no longer felt like a place of growth, nourishment, or encounter with Christ.

Some found what they were missing in Protestant denominations. In the same Pew survey, 70 percent of respondents said they left "because they found a religion they like more." Many who left the church point to stronger preaching, a clearer invitation into a personal relationship with Jesus, or a worship environment that felt more alive and emotionally engaging. Others found deeper connections in small groups, accountability relationships, or a sense of intentional community. For many, it wasn't about rejecting Catholic belief; it was about seeking a spiritual experience they didn't feel they were receiving where they were.

In many surveys I reviewed, those who left the Church cited uninspiring worship, lack of spiritual growth, or a lack of spiritual support from their parish community. That's not easy to hear, but it's something we have to take seriously. Most aren't rejecting Christianity outright; they're looking for a faith that feels real and personal.

As I reflected on this, I found myself asking: *What kind of spiritual nourishment do I long for most, and where have I experienced it since coming back to the Church?* For me, it's been in showing up, not just for Mass, but for everything my parish offers. Bible studies. Men's groups. Monthly fellowship meals. Local Catholic retreats. Archdiocesan events. These are the things that have helped me grow, re-engage, and begin to experience the depth that has always been present in the Church, even if it took me years to find my way back to it.

CULTURAL PRESSURES AND SECULAR INFLUENCES

Let's face it—the world has changed dramatically in recent decades, and it's not slowing down. Technology, in particular, has reshaped how we live, think, and relate. As I reviewed the data on why Catholics leave the Church for this chapter, one thing became clear: cultural pressures and the influence of modern secularism weigh heavily, especially on younger generations. Three things distinctly stood out to me.

First is the spread of a secular worldview. Faith can seem optional or even unimportant in a culture driven by material success and self-fulfillment. Over time, this mindset often leads to a lack of engagement. One Pew study noted that for every person who joins the Catholic Church in the U.S., more than eight leave it. That data came from 2015, and although the picture showed only slight improvement for several years, more recent reports suggest the trend may finally be slowing, with signs that departures are leveling off and new conversions are beginning to rise.

Second, shifting moral and social values play a major role. As I noted earlier in this chapter, many Catholics have left because they no longer agree with Church teachings, particularly on issues like abortion, sexuality, and gender. These teachings often conflict with cultural norms and the personal values of friends and family. That tension can be difficult, sometimes impossible, for people to reconcile.

Finally, there's the media, especially social media. The digital world delivers a nonstop stream of news, opinions, and commentary, often amplifying the Church's failures and portraying it in the worst possible light. Headlines and sound bites travel faster than truth or context, and stories of scandal or division tend to drown out the witness of faithful priests, religious, and lay people. For many, especially younger adults, this has eroded trust and made disengagement feel easier or even justified. At the same time, those platforms that spread doubt can also spread hope, offering reminders that the Church is still alive and vibrant in ways the broader culture often overlooks.

Secularism, moral shifts, and media influence don't tell the whole story. But together they've created a climate where staying connected to Catholic life requires more intention than ever before. But there's another kind of struggle. One that does not come from the outside. We'll turn to that next.

WOUNDS FROM WITHIN THE CHURCH—
THE ABUSE CRISIS

Note: The following section includes a discussion of the Church's sexual abuse crisis. If you've experienced trauma connected to this, please read with care. My hope is to name this wound honestly and with compassion, while still keeping our eyes on Christ.

We couldn't write a chapter on why people leave the Catholic Church without acknowledging the harm caused by the sexual abuse crisis and its impact on victims, their families, and the broader Church community. This was a global tragedy that unfolded over decades. The abuse itself was devastating. In many cases, the institutional response, particularly the documented mishandling of reports, only deepened the suffering. In this section, I want to make space for honesty, grief, and reflection while keeping our focus on Christ. If those affected ever return to the Church, it will be a return to *Him*.

This wound is difficult and painful to name, much less revisit. For many Catholics and their families, it wasn't just a scandal; it was a profound spiritual betrayal. This wasn't just a headline; it was deeply personal. It shattered trust, isolated victims, and left communities grieving and disoriented. Some walked away from the Church, but not from God. Many still believe, but the institution no longer feels safe or trustworthy. The pain has affected survivors, their families, regular parishioners, and even those who stayed in the Church but didn't know how to respond. Much of the institutional side of this crisis has already been covered in news reports, legal investigations, and official Church statements, and it is familiar to most readers.

While I'm not an expert on abuse policy within the Catholic Church, I've spent nearly 35 years in child welfare, including 30 years in public child protection at the state level. Early in my career, I worked directly with victims and families, often within child welfare systems under immense pressure. Later on, I oversaw programs across an entire state system, and the harm I witnessed could at times feel overwhelming. I've seen what abuse does to victims and families, and I know how long the healing process truly takes. My experience as a child welfare professional and as a practicing Catholic informs my approach to this topic. Wounds like these do not simply disappear. They call for truth, justice, accountability, and time.

This crisis has cost us dearly. The harm done to individuals and families cannot be overstated. It also caused many to lose confidence in the Church, not just in its leaders, but in its ability to protect and respond with care and compassion. Some Catholics left quietly. Others left in pain or anger. Many have never come back. In some cases, the Church's response felt distant or uncertain, leaving people with more questions than peace. For some, this was the moment the Church no longer felt like home. It became a source of pain.

And yet, in the middle of all this, many Catholics stayed. Some even came back. Not because they forgot what happened, but because their faith still meant something real. Some talk about their love for the Eucharist. Others say it was the grace of Confession or the people in their parish who helped them keep going. The sacraments became a steady place to land when so much else felt broken. Their faith didn't excuse the harm. It gave them a way to endure it.

Still, for many people, healing has taken time and space. I don't have easy answers, but I can say this: if you've been hurt, I understand. And if you're ever ready to come back, you're not alone. When someone considers returning to their Catholic faith, it's not about going back to an institution that once failed them. It's a return to Christ and *His Church*, not to perfect people or faultless leaders. It's a return not to what went wrong but to the One who remains faithful.

We must believe that healing is possible. And some who were wounded have found it, not by forgetting what happened, but by grounding themselves more deeply in Christ. Others are still in the middle of that journey. And many may never return. However, the Church cannot move forward without real reform and a commitment to truth. We know this. Even so, Jesus is still here. He has never stopped offering comfort, presence, and hope. Even in our deepest wounds, Christ is present. He may not erase the pain, but He walks with us through it.

WHAT HAPPENS WHEN WE STEP AWAY

It was only when God called me back to my Catholic faith that I fully grasped the impact of leaving and the loss it created in my life. Looking back on the 40 years I was away, there were consequences. While I was mostly happy during those years, I always carried a lingering sense that something important was missing. I knew, deep down, that I longed for a closer connection with God. But it took time to understand that what I was missing was rooted in the Catholic faith. I couldn't always see it then.

The sacraments are how Catholics stay rooted in God's grace. Without them, something essential to our spiritual life quietly slips away. As I reflect on this now, I believe that the Eucharist might be the most significant loss we experience when we fall away from the Church. The Eucharist is described in the Catechism as "the source and summit of the Christian life" *(Catechism of the Catholic Church, 2nd ed., 1324)*. Without it, we miss out on the gift that unites us both physically and spiritually with Christ. It's the food we need for the challenges of daily life. When we go without it, the emptiness sets in, and it feels like something essential is missing from both our faith and our connection with God.

The Sacrament of Reconciliation is another significant loss we face. Confession is not just about forgiveness; it's also about healing the wounds that sin leaves behind. When we step away from the Church, we lose access to this spiritual healing that we need throughout our journey. Without it, feelings of guilt, regret, and separation from God can linger for years, unresolved.

There's also an impact that reaches beyond the individual. We don't often discuss it, but when someone leaves the Church, whether they are a parent or may become one, it can create a spiritual gap that is passed on to the next generation. This becomes a *second wave of loss*. Children raised outside the Catholic faith may miss out on the sacraments of initiation: Baptism, Confirmation, the Eucharist, and the grace that accompanies each of them. The Church also provides us with a clear moral and spiritual framework for living our lives. When that's missing, something vital is lost.

Alongside the family impact, there was something else I didn't fully recognize until I came back—the overlooked loss of Catholic community. I often sensed something else was missing during those years, even when I attended Protestant churches. It wasn't that those churches lacked fellowship. They offered plenty. What I didn't realize I was missing until I returned was the shared life of the Catholic Church: its prayers, the rhythm of the liturgy, and the sense of community in parish life. For those who leave, that loss may not be immediately apparent. But over time, the absence of that spiritual grounding and sacramental life can leave a hidden gap that's hard to name.

Even after returning to my faith, I've still felt a sense of regret. When I left the Church as I was heading off to college, I didn't just miss the sacraments. I also lost the chance to be the spiritual leader my future family would need, and that's something I carry with me. It didn't have to be that way. But even so, there's great joy in what can be *regained* when a fallen-away Catholic comes home. Through Confession, our relationship with God is healed and restored. Through the Eucharist, we are given new strength and a renewed connection to Christ, just the way He intended. The transformation I've experienced has been remarkable. Returning to the Church has deepened my appreciation for its rich history, its teachings, the sacraments, and the role it plays in my journey toward salvation.

Yet even with all of this, there is great hope. I'll talk more about that next. The memories I carry from my Catholic upbringing, including the rituals and traditions, have taken on new life since my return. What I've believed all my life has become clearer, grounded in Catholic teaching and the strength of God's word. I regret leaving the Church, but that time away is now part of my story, and something that continues to shape how I live out my Christian faith today.

A MESSAGE OF HOPE

When I meet Catholics who have left the Church, talk with parents whose adult children no longer attend Mass, or reflect on my own time away, I remain hopeful. If I could return, there's hope that anyone can.

I want to fully acknowledge that the pain, doubt, or distance some people feel is real. But even so, it's never too late to come back. The door is always open. Christ welcomes us, no matter how long it's been. The Church is not here to keep people out, but to open the way for all to experience God's love and grace.

You don't need to have it all figured out before taking the first step. I certainly didn't. I returned with questions, with hesitation, and with a few lingering doubts. But I took a step anyway. For some, that step might be attending Mass again. For others, it may be as simple as saying a prayer, reading Scripture, or talking with a priest. Often, it's in these small moments that we begin to remember just how deeply God loves us and start to feel drawn back to the faith. It isn't only meant to be understood intellectually. It's meant to be experienced. Sometimes God teaches us not through ideas. He teaches through the moments and people He places in front of us.

Many of us wrestle with a common misunderstanding—that returning to the Church means having it all together. Some feel there's a standard of perfection they'll never meet, as if they need to attend daily Mass or never doubt again to "do it right." But that's not how grace works. The goal isn't perfection; it's an ongoing and developing relationship with Christ. And like any real relationship, it grows over time through small steps, humility, and love. When we expect perfect faith, whether in ourselves or others, it often leads to disappointment and distraction.

Part of this pressure can sometimes come from well-meaning voices online. I've followed many Catholic influencers on YouTube, Instagram, and podcasts, and several have been important in my own return to the Church. However, even with the best intentions, these voices can occasionally present an image of the faith that feels too perfect and may be overwhelming. It's easy to walk away from a post or video and believe we're not doing enough, or that we'll never measure up. That's when we have to gently remind ourselves that faith isn't about someone else's path, but about our own walk with Christ.

God doesn't call us to be flawless. He calls us to be faithful and to follow him. And that often starts with simply showing up.

If you've been away for a while, you don't have to rush or try to make up for lost time. I fell into that trap early on, thinking I had to prove something or catch up. But the truth is, you can begin wherever you are, with whatever faith you have today. The sacraments, scripture, prayer, and parish life are all there to support you. But it starts with Jesus. He's not waiting for a polished, perfected version of you. He's waiting for *you*. As you begin the journey back, you'll realize your return isn't defined by religious performance but by grace, which meets us exactly where we are.

As I shared in Chapter 1, my return to the Church has been nothing short of life-changing. I'm not the same person I was before. Every journey is different, of course, but I've come to believe the peace, purpose, and healing that follow a return to faith will change your life, just as they have mine. When we find our way home, we begin to love God and others in a new way—more fully, more freely, and more like Christ.

Along the way, I've been encouraged by the stories of others who've returned to the Church or entered it for the first time. We often use labels like convert, revert, cradle Catholic, or fallen away, and I understand why. But sometimes, those terms feel like they put us in separate categories when, in truth, we're all just trying to follow Christ. One of the people I've learned the most from is my wife. A few years ago, she had the courage to step into the Church for the first time as I returned to my faith. Watching her discover Catholicism with fresh eyes, after growing up Protestant, has helped me see things in a new way, too. Her journey has been a gift and a reminder that no matter how we arrive, we're all invited into the same love and grace from God. The honesty and courage I've seen in others have shaped my own journey more than they probably realize. They've reminded me that the Church is not just a place we come back to, it's a home that is always calling people in.

I wrote this book because I know I'm not alone. There are many others like me—people who walked away, people who aren't sure how to come back, and those who love someone who's left. If that's you, I want to encourage you to take that first step. Even if it's a simple one, take it. Let go of whatever is holding you back, and trust that God will guide you home.

3

Taking the First Step
The Courage to Reach Out

LOOKING BACK AT MY return, I can tell you it wasn't easy. As I shared in chapter 1, I felt drawn back to the Church long before I went back to Mass. But I wasn't sure what I was being called to do. Was it a call to return to my Catholic faith? A call to grow closer to Jesus? A call to leave behind sin? Maybe it was all three. What I do know is that it took time and courage to take that first step. For me, it had been forty years. For you, it might be less, or even more. Either way, this chapter is about what that step can look like and some of the challenges you might face when you feel the nudge to come back.

COMMON WORRIES ABOUT RETURNING

Let's face it, if you were raised Catholic and have been away for a while, returning can stir up real anxiety. When I've told this to people who became Catholic, they're often surprised. But I think it's something unique to former Catholics. There may be many reasons for it, but I've come to believe it's a real barrier for many who feel called back. The fear I felt about going to Mass for the first time in decades definitely *held me* back. I worried about being judged or feeling like I didn't belong anymore. I was anxious about not knowing the order of the Mass, the prayers, or even how to behave. It had been forty years, after all. I also carried guilt, not just for leaving the Church, but for some of the choices I had made while I was away from God. I still hold some of that, but God's grace is helping me let it go.

When I sat at Mass for the first time in all those years, I remember thanking God in the silence of my heart for calling me home. I still thank him for that. But even in that moment, I felt uncertainty. I wasn't sure I knew enough, even though I'd grown up Catholic. And I wasn't sure I believed enough—not just in the Church's teachings, but in whether I was even worthy to return. Would God forgive me for walking away? Had it been too long? These are common thoughts, and I've come to learn they're all part of the journey. Over time, I began to understand that God's love is bigger than any sin, and his forgiveness is *always* waiting for us. Knowing this still overwhelms me at times.

There may also be some social discomfort. I experienced this myself, and I see it often in others, both in returning Catholics and in those who convert. It's normal to feel anxious about how others might see you. Maybe your friends or family don't understand this pull you're feeling. Perhaps you worry about what other parishioners think. You might feel embarrassed that you don't remember the flow of the Mass or the prayers. I've felt all of that too. But most of the time, the people around us aren't judging us at all. They're likely just curious about your story, or even about the faith itself. And the people in your parish? Most of them will simply be glad you're there. They will want to walk with you, not watch from a distance.

My advice is to focus on your relationship with God first. That's where everything begins and where it all returns. Don't worry about having all the answers or knowing exactly what to do next. Just be honest about what's happening within you. What is God inviting you to notice, to let go of, or to move toward? Try to stay rooted in that call, your path, not someone else's. There are plenty of resources to help you relearn the Mass, prayers, and aspects of Catholic life, but those are just tools. They matter, *but they aren't the heart of your return.* The heart of it is your desire to say yes to God again. So don't let fear or unfamiliarity keep you stuck. Begin with a simple prayer. Show up for Mass. Ask for help if you need it. Just take the next step, and trust that God will meet you there.

What helps is remembering that you're not alone. I felt all of these things when I returned, and so do many others. Just keep in mind, this is *your* journey. You can only walk your path, not anyone else's. And don't forget, our Church has been around for two thousand years. It's not perfect. It was never meant to be. The Church isn't for people who have it all together. It's for sinners who are trying to follow Christ. God will meet you in the reality of today if you come with honesty and humility. You don't need polished answers. A willing heart is enough.

ATTENDING MASS AGAIN

For me, everything started here, in the simple act of returning to Mass after years away. However, this might also be the most challenging step to take. No matter how long it's been, returning can feel awkward or unfamiliar. And if you're returning to a parish where people might recognize you, that can bring up added emotions. For others, it may have been so long that the parish feels entirely new. Either way, it helps to remember what brought you there. Take it in small steps. For me, it had been forty years. I had to give myself permission to be a beginner again. In those early days, I kept coming back to one simple truth: I was there to renew my relationship with Jesus.

If you're unsure about where you stand in your return to the Church, I encourage you to still come to Mass. Just come. For that first time back, go easy on yourself. Sit in a back pew if that helps. Let yourself be still. No pressure or expectations.

I think the structure of the Mass is where many returning Catholics can feel overwhelmed or distracted. If it's been a while, the rhythm might feel off or even confusing. I know it did for me.

At first, I felt completely lost. For those first few Masses, just kneel and stand with the congregation. If your parish provides a missalette or other worship book, use it to follow along during the service. If not, you can look up the basic flow of the Mass online. There are also several apps that walk you through the Mass and the prayers. I used one of those early on.

In the broadest sense, the Mass consists of four main parts. First are the *Introductory Rites*, which include the Penitential Act, the Gloria, and an opening prayer. Next comes the Liturgy of the Word: the first reading, followed by the responsorial psalm, then the second reading, the Alleluia, and finally the proclamation of the Gospel. After that, the priest or deacon offers the homily, a brief reflection on the readings. Some people might know it as the sermon. This is also when we recite the Nicene Creed (or occasionally the Apostles' Creed). The heart of the Mass is the *Liturgy of the Eucharist*, also known as Holy Communion. Finally, the *Concluding Rites* bring the Mass to a close with a final blessing and dismissal. The priest or deacon says something like, "Go in peace," and we respond, "Thanks be to God." Many people remain for a few moments of prayer before leaving, so it's thoughtful to step outside for conversations after Mass.

This is just a basic overview, but it can help you find your footing in the beginning. For a more detailed guide, I personally use and recommend *The New Saint Joseph Missal*, the complete edition. It includes all the daily readings, as well as a full Order of Mass and prayers. I'm not a liturgical expert, just someone who's been through the process of returning and wanted a straightforward way to follow along. Mine is divided into three volumes: two for weekday Masses and a separate one for Sundays. I used it as a reference for the summary above, and it's played a small but steady part in my return to the Church. It also happens to be the same missal my mother used when I was a kid, so holding it again brings a sense of comfort—like a link between the past and the present.

When you've been away a long time, it's easy to get caught up in the details. You might worry about when to kneel, when to pray, or how to respond. That's understandable. But don't let the form distract you from the purpose. You didn't return just to recite the right words. You came back because something has been waking up inside you. You came to be near God again. The beauty of the Mass is that it will become familiar again over time. For now, just focus on being present. The details will come. What matters most is why you walked through those doors. Just being there is enough.

There will be a moment during Mass when the congregation receives Holy Communion. As Catholics, this is when we are closest to Christ, receiving him as he intended. But if you've been away for some time, you may need to wait before receiving the Eucharist, especially if you haven't yet spoken with a priest or gone to confession. I'll talk more about that in the next section. For now, it's essential to understand the Church's teaching: "Anyone conscious of a grave sin must receive the sacrament of Reconciliation before coming to communion." (*Catechism of the Catholic Church*, 2nd ed., 1385).

We're asked to examine our conscience, go to confession, and be in a state of grace before receiving Holy Communion. A priest can help guide you through that process.

But even if you're not yet ready to receive the Eucharist, you can still take part in the moment. While you're always welcome to stay in your pew if that is more comfortable, I'd encourage you to come forward in the Communion line with your arms crossed over your chest. This is a traditional way to request a blessing from a priest or deacon. I received blessings for several months before I went to confession and received the Eucharist again. And even then, those simple blessings were meaningful to me. It was just another moment where I felt God calling me closer.

My final piece of advice for those first few times you attend Mass is this: try to meet a few people. I know that's not easy. I'm an introvert myself, so it doesn't come naturally to me either. When I first returned to Mass in the small town where we now live, I was fortunate that Mary Beth and I recognized a few familiar faces from the community, and they were genuinely glad to see us. In a smaller parish, people are more likely to notice visitors, and some will come up and introduce themselves. The more people you meet early on, the easier it becomes to step more fully into parish life if you decide to keep coming back.

And if someone invites you to an event after Mass, like a parish breakfast or a Bible study, go—even if it feels a little uncomfortable. Not long after I returned, Mary Beth and I were invited to an adult education gathering after church, and it turned out to be one of the best things we did. Many of those people are now close friends at our parish. My point is this: don't miss those early opportunities. That might be the way God is gently leading you forward.

If you're feeling worried or anxious about returning to Mass, you might consider watching an online Mass first. These became more common during the COVID pandemic and made the liturgy accessible to many during that time. While online Mass can never take the place of attending in person, it might be a helpful starting point if you're truly anxious about going back, or if you simply want to supplement in-person attendance as you relearn the Order of the Mass, the prayers, and the overall flow. Websites like CatholicTV, EWTN, and Mass-Online.org stream daily and Sunday Masses from churches across the country, which can be a good resource in the early days of your return.

TAKING THE NEXT STEP: MEETING WITH A PRIEST

No matter how long you've been away from the Church, I always recommend speaking with a priest early on. It's often one of the first concrete steps in your return, and it can be a meaningful part of discerning what comes next. Returning to the Church is personal, but you don't have to walk that road alone. A priest can help provide clarity on next steps, answer your questions, and provide spiritual guidance if needed. And because he's part of your local parish, he can speak directly to your situation. There's something reassuring about sitting across from someone who listens with compassion and understanding during this early stage.

Taking the First Step

This step was difficult for me. And honestly, a little scary. I hadn't had a one-on-one conversation with a priest since before I left for college. I had questions, but I didn't do a great job preparing. So my first piece of advice is this: prepare better than I did! Find a quiet space and pray beforehand. Ask the Lord to guide your thoughts and help you bring up questions with openness and trust.

Scheduling the meeting is usually simple. Most parishes list the priest's contact information on their website. If you attend a larger parish, consider calling the church office to schedule through their staff. However, I found it easier to email the priest directly. That gave me time to share a bit of my own story, how long I'd been away, and that I was thinking about returning to the Church.

You can expect the conversation to be warm and welcoming. Remember, this isn't a test, and there's no need to rush. Be ready to share your story: how you were raised Catholic, what led you away, and why you feel called to return. It's also a good time to ask questions. I had been away for so long that I needed clarity on a few basic things—issues I hadn't thought about in years. I wanted to understand how the Church approaches difficult or sensitive topics these days with both truth and compassion. It's perfectly fine to ask questions that might feel awkward.

Confession may also come up. In my case, I brought it up first. I told my priest I hadn't been to confession in over forty years and that I was ready to make a confession that day. He gently encouraged me to take more time, to sit with it, pray, and do a thorough examination of conscience. Looking back, that was the best advice he could have given me. I needed time to understand the sacrament again, and to prepare well. There are plenty of resources available, including apps that guide you through the process. We'll talk more about confession in a later chapter, but for now, just take your time. Reconciliation is about returning fully to God's grace, and that kind of return deserves time and reflection.

If you're married, be sure to let the priest know. But he'll likely ask. Share how long you've been married and where the ceremony took place: whether in another church, at the courthouse, or by someone else authorized to officiate in your state. I'll go deeper into marriage-related considerations in a later chapter, but it's important to bring this up early, since it often comes into play.

Marriage and divorce can be complicated, and every story is different. If you were married outside the Catholic Church, which is very common among returning Catholics, you may need to go through a process called *convalidation*. I discuss this further in chapter 5, but in short, convalidation is the Church's process for recognizing your marriage as a sacrament by having you exchange your marriage vows in the Catholic Church. Other situations may come up, too: divorce, remarriage, or being married to someone who wasn't baptized Catholic. I'm not an expert in this area, but I've learned that the Church approaches these conversations with care and compassion. Your priest will help you understand what applies in your case and walk with you through it.

And don't forget to ask about the next steps and what kind of support the Church offers as you return. In many parishes, you'll be invited to attend the *Order of Christian Initiation of Adults* (OCIA), which is also known as RCIA. While OCIA is typically associated with those entering the Church for the first time, like unbaptized adults or Christians from other denominations, it can also be very helpful for returning Catholics. I went through RCIA with my wife, Mary Beth, who was coming into the Church for the first time. Even if you've only been away for a few years, OCIA provides a solid way to reacquaint yourself with Church teaching, connect with others, and deepen your understanding of the faith and your local parish life. I now recommend that all Catholics consider attending OCIA every 3–5 years if your parish allows it.

A few final tips. *Be honest.* You don't need to have everything figured out, and it's okay if you're unsure where this will lead. Just be open about your situation. *Bring your questions*, even if they feel unorganized. And *pray beforehand*. I said this earlier, but it's worth repeating—asking God to guide your words and your heart can change everything. Even a simple prayer like "God, help me to be open" is enough.

If you haven't prayed in a while, don't worry. That's exactly what we'll talk about next.

TAKING THE FIRST STEP

RECONNECTING WITH PRAYER

Prayer is an area in which many of us struggle—myself included. So don't feel pressured to rush this part of your return. Reconnecting with prayer is a process that you'll continue to grow and deepen throughout your life. It doesn't have to be perfect. It doesn't have to be long. Think of it as returning to a conversation that never really ended, a conversation with the Lord.

Even if you haven't prayed in years, you've probably prayed more than you realize. Perhaps in moments of gratitude, in fear, or when facing something challenging. Maybe you felt a gentle nudge while driving, or stood in awe of a sunset and sensed the presence of something greater. That, too, is prayer. It may not have looked like the formal prayers you learned growing up, but God hears all of it. The door was never closed.

This section is about walking through that door again and learning to see prayer with fresh eyes.

There are many helpful resources out there. I think that reacquainting yourself with the *daily readings* of the Church is a great place to start. These are short Scripture passages chosen for each day of the year, used in Masses worldwide. Whether you're sitting in a small parish or a large cathedral, the same readings are being read that day. It's one of the beautiful ways we stay connected as a Church. I recommend subscribing to the daily email from the *United States Conference of Catholic Bishops (USCCB)*. I read them first thing in the morning. You can listen to the readings as you follow along, and there's also a brief video reflection that you can watch.

I've already mentioned the *St. Joseph Missal*, which includes the daily readings and several beautiful prayers. The *Magnificat* is another great option, a daily Mass companion with readings, reflections, and stories about the saints. An additional helpful book I've come to appreciate is the *Catholic Book of Prayers*. It includes many classic Catholic prayers, the full Order of the Mass, and a guide for doing a good examination of conscience before confession.

There are also many prayer apps, including *Hallow*, *Laudate*, and *iBreviary*. Each one is a little different, but all help guide prayer, the rosary, and daily Scripture meditations. All of these tools can be useful, but never forget that the most essential form of prayer is simply that one-on-one time with God. Just sitting in silence each day, perhaps with Scripture, but more importantly, with a heart that listens. If we listen closely enough, God always speaks. Maybe through Scripture. Maybe through others. Maybe in the stillness of your own soul. What matters is that you come with an open heart.

Relearning foundational prayers, such as the Our Father (the Lord's Prayer), the Hail Mary, and the Act of Contrition, can help you establish or reestablish a rhythm of prayer. I say the Our Father and Hail Mary together each day. If you're just starting to develop a habit, begin with one prayer before or after your daily readings. You can also pray during ordinary moments, such as while driving, walking, or lying in bed. Most people would say that morning is the best time to pray, and I'd have to agree. The beginning of the day is the perfect time to offer your day to the Lord, to ask not just for help with your needs or for the people in your life, but for the grace to be a stronger disciple for Him. It's perfectly fine to speak to God as you would a friend.

Evening prayer can be a time of gratitude, thanking God for the day, asking forgiveness for where we've fallen short, and asking Him to bless us so we can do better tomorrow.

Praying with others is important too—at Mass, with your spouse, or in a small group. It deepens your connection not just to God, but to the people around you. And don't forget prayers at mealtime. That small act of giving thanks before eating can become a powerful reminder that even the simple things, like a meal with your family, are gifts from Him.

There will be times when prayer is spontaneous and simple, and others when more structured or traditional prayers feel right. While prayer is always a conversation with God, learning to pray the Rosary, the Divine Mercy Chaplet (often prayed using a rosary), or using a method like Lectio Divina can deepen your relationship with God. I won't go into detail here, but I encourage you to take some time to explore these. Each offers a unique way to slow down, reflect, and enter into meaningful time with the Lord.

And finally, consider Eucharistic Adoration, the practice of spending quiet time before the Blessed Sacrament—the consecrated host. It's one of the most powerful ways to pray, reflect, or simply sit in the presence of Jesus. I don't recall Adoration being offered in my parish when I was younger. Perhaps it was, but it wasn't something I ever encountered. After returning to the faith, I began taking part more consistently, encouraged by my priest. My parish offers Adoration after Thursday Mass, and I try to attend as often as I can. I've found that spending 45–60 minutes there is a powerful time for reflection and for preparing my heart for confession with a thorough examination of conscience.

Whatever form your prayer takes, remember to go slowly. Ask for God's grace. Many Catholics, even those who have practiced their entire lives, often feel distracted or believe that nothing is happening. That's okay. It doesn't mean you're doing anything wrong, so try not to get discouraged. Sometimes just showing up, even when it feels dry, is the most faithful prayer of all. Whether you start with one simple prayer in the morning or eventually find yourself in silent Adoration, what matters is that you've turned back toward God.

As your prayer life begins to take root again, it re-centers your focus and helps prepare you for the next step forward in faith.

MOVING FORWARD IN FAITH

Once you decide to return to your Catholic faith and begin attending Mass regularly, you might expect everything to settle into place. And in some ways, it will. But other parts might still feel hard. In this section, I want to take an honest look at what happens next, not just the visible steps, but the feelings that often come with them. Where do you turn for support when it gets tough? And how do you carry your faith into the everyday moments of your life?

The first reality you might face is that not everyone will understand. And that's okay. You may feel the support of your parish community, your priest, and even some family and friends. But others might not know what to make of your return, especially if it comes with a new level of conviction or joy that surprises them. I experienced this myself, and to be honest, I still do sometimes. For a long time, I kept God's pull on my heart private. But when I returned, I came back with energy and openness about my faith, and not everyone knew what to do with that. Some people responded with indifference, while others responded with polite skepticism, and in a few cases, even with discomfort. That can happen, even with those closest to you.

When it does, remind yourself that you don't owe anyone an explanation. This is *your* walk with Christ, no one else's. Don't get defensive if uncomfortable conversations come up. Be clear about your call to return, and be kind and gentle if others ask questions. You can use those moments to share what you're learning or to clarify a few things about the Catholic faith. But sometimes people may not want to engage at all, and that's okay too.

You might also face some resistance from within. As you return to regular prayer, it's not unusual to go through dry spells or to see old habits start creeping back in. Sometimes prayer will feel flat or distracted. You might sit down with good intentions and feel nothing. No peace or clarity. Just silence. That's okay. Spiritual dryness isn't a failure; it's a natural part of the journey. Even the saints wrote about it. God is still present in that silence. Your willingness to show up anyway is, in itself, a powerful act of faith. Doubts may arise. You might even begin to question your decision to return. If you feel yourself slipping, know that this is part of the journey. Be patient. As much as God is working to draw you closer, the enemy is always looking for ways to pull you away from grace. That's not something to fear, but it is something to be aware of. Growth in faith isn't always steady—it can feel messy or winding at times. That doesn't mean you're doing something wrong. It may actually mean you're doing something right. Faith isn't about perfection. It's about showing up, especially when it's hard.

If you still find yourself wrestling with Church teachings, don't let that stop you from moving forward. You can return to your

Taking the First Step

Catholic faith even if you're not sure where you stand on everything. Faith doesn't begin with full intellectual agreement. It starts with trust. With relationship. With a heart that says, "I want to know You more, Lord." That kind of honesty is a good place to start.

You're allowed to ask questions. You're allowed to take your time. No one expects you to understand it all—not even God. And most of us never do. If something feels confusing or unsettled, bring it to prayer. Talk with your priest or someone else you trust who has a solid understanding of Scripture and the Church's teachings. Find out what the Church truly teaches, not just what you've heard secondhand. Consider reading the Catechism, not to memorize doctrine, but to better grasp the meaning behind it.

In my experience, clarity came slowly and unfolded over time, through quiet moments, Scripture, and conversations with my wife or others in my Bible study group. There were times I still didn't fully understand. But I stayed close to Jesus, and that made all the difference. So keep going. Stay curious and ask questions. God is never afraid of them. And the Church isn't either.

Someone once said to me, "Being Catholic isn't just a religion, it's a way of life." And I've found that to be true. It shapes how you interact with others, how you manage your finances, the type of content you consume, and how you respond when life becomes challenging. It shows up in the choices you make when no one's watching. This, too, is part of discipleship.

Let your return begin to shape how you live, not just on Sundays, but in the routines of daily life. Stay close to the sacraments. Make prayer a regular habit. Be intentional about the voices you listen to, the words you use, and how you spend your time.

Service is another powerful expression of your faith. Volunteering at your parish or helping those in need within your community is a beautiful way to live out your beliefs. I'll talk more about finding your way in your parish in an upcoming chapter.

And don't forget the virtues. Practice patience, mercy, forgiveness, and love. Not perfectly, but faithfully. Keep visual reminders of your faith around you—a crucifix, a Bible, a daily devotional. They don't need to be flashy, just visible enough to keep you rooted when the world starts to tug at your attention. Your Catholic faith doesn't have to be loud to be real. But it should be visible. Be a quiet beacon of hope in your home, workplace, or community. You never know who's watching, and your example may matter more than you think.

As we close this chapter on taking those first steps in your return, remember that small steps matter too. You don't have to leap. Just take the next small, faithful step. That could mean praying before bed, joining a parish Bible study, or simply showing up to Mass even when you don't feel like it. Surround yourself with people and practices that nourish your faith—Mass, the sacraments, Scripture, and prayer. And if you haven't already, I highly recommend attending the *Order of Christian Initiation of Adults (OCIA)*. It's one of the best ways to grow in your understanding of Church teaching, the sacraments, and how to live your faith with confidence. When I returned, I was the only one in our OCIA group who came back to the Church after being away. But it didn't matter. I had just as many questions as those coming into the Church for the first time, and the experience helped deepen my understanding and strengthen my faith.

Beyond the learning, OCIA can also be a place for connection. You'll meet others who are asking the same kinds of questions, even if their paths to the Church look different from yours. I learned so much from the questions Mary Beth was asking throughout the process. Such shared experiences can be both grounding and encouraging.

You've already said yes—now let your return be a journey, not just a moment. Take time to walk it slowly, and let God's grace meet you along the way. One of the most critical steps in this journey is returning to the Sacrament of Reconciliation, which we'll explore in the next chapter.

4

Reconciliation
Embracing a Fresh Start

I MENTIONED IN THE last chapter that attending Mass for the first time in many years is often the first concrete step on the way home. And that's true. But making your first confession after a long absence is different. It's deeper and more personal. It may feel like the most profound step you'll take in your first year back in the Church. It's also necessary. If sin is what separates us from God, then Reconciliation is what heals that separation. This sacrament restores grace and brings us back into full communion with God and with the Church that He calls us to belong to.

Next to the Eucharist, this is the sacrament that keeps me Catholic. It's a gift that Christ gave us—not as a burden, but as a path forward. A way to be forgiven and maintain spiritual health. A way to be close to Him, not just in belief, but in genuine friendship.

I'm not a theologian or a Church scholar. I'm just a Catholic who came back after a long time away, and I've walked the path you're on now. What I've written here reflects what I've come to understand through reading, through conversations, and through my own experience of returning to the sacrament. None of this is theory for me. I've tried to stay faithful to what the Church teaches, but I'm not speaking from a place of authority. I'm writing as someone who knows what it's like to feel uncertain and vulnerable. And I've come to believe that God's grace is present in those very places—in our doubts, our struggles, and our fears.

WHAT IS THE SACRAMENT OF RECONCILIATION?

The Sacrament of Reconciliation, also known as Penance and Confession, is one of the seven sacraments of the Catholic Church. This sacrament, like the others, was instituted by Jesus Christ to bring us forgiveness for sins committed since baptism. Put simply, Reconciliation lets us seek forgiveness, heal our relationship with God, and be restored to communion with the Church.

It's not just about clearing the slate, but about receiving grace that strengthens us going forward. This sacrament allows us to begin again, not just privately, but also in communion with the Church. While it goes by many names, I believe that "Reconciliation" is the name that makes the most sense and best reflects its intent: a return, a restoration, and the healing that comes through forgiveness.

Not long after I returned to the Church, someone in my family who had stopped practicing years earlier asked me a question that stayed with me. Why do we need to go to a priest for confession? Why not just tell God we're sorry, directly and privately? At the time, I didn't have a perfect answer, but I understood where the question was coming from. I had wondered the same thing myself.

Now, when someone asks me that question, I usually answer by saying, "Because Jesus set it up this way." What I mean is that the Sacrament of Reconciliation was part of His plan from the beginning. He gave the apostles the authority to forgive sins, as seen in the Gospel of John (20:21–23), where He breathed on them and said that if they forgive the sins of others, those sins are forgiven. That same authority has been passed down through the Church for centuries, through bishops and priests.

When I returned to the Church, one of my biggest questions before confession was about sin, what it is, and how the Church defines it. Before we proceed in this chapter, I would like to pause and provide some straightforward definitions.

Mortal sin is the most serious kind of sin. It's when someone knowingly and freely chooses a grave act against God's law—one that breaks our communion with Him. Not every sin falls into this category. A sin only separates us from God if it is grave in nature and chosen with full awareness and freedom. The Catechism explains that mortal sin involves grave matter, full knowledge, and deliberate consent (*Catechism of the Catholic Church*, 2nd ed., 1857).

Venial sins are the more ordinary sins we commit in daily life. These include things like pride, impatience, or gossip. While venial sins don't cut us off from God entirely, they do weaken our relationship with Him. If left unaddressed, they can make us more vulnerable to falling into more serious sins over time.

There will be times when you're not sure what kind of sin something is, and that's okay. There are plenty of good resources out there that can help, and I've found the *Catechism of the Catholic Church* to be one of the best places to start.

If I were to sum up my feelings about the Sacrament of Reconciliation, it comes down to hope and mercy. There is hope for all of us to receive God's mercy and to begin again. His mercy is far greater than any sin we could ever commit. Just remember that Reconciliation isn't about punishment. It's about God's mercy. When we open our hearts to it, we begin to live with more freedom, more trust, and a more profound sense of belonging to Him.

MY FIRST TIME BACK

At first, I wasn't sure if I should include the story of my first confession after forty years away from the Church. It wasn't part of my original outline for this chapter. I wondered if it would be too personal, or if it might take away from the focus on helping others understand the sacrament itself. But the more I sat with it, the more I realized how much it might help. If sharing my experience helps ease fear, settle the anxiety that builds after years away, or clear up confusion about what to expect, then it belongs here. The truth is, most people returning to the Church don't need a complete manual on Reconciliation. They need to hear from someone who's been there. Someone who knows what it's like to walk in with nerves, doubts, or even dread and walk out feeling forgiven and relieved.

In the last chapter, I mentioned that when I met with a priest for the first time, I thought I was ready to make my confession that day. I wasn't. Looking back now, I can see that I wasn't even close. At that point in my reversion, I wasn't in the right frame of mind to fully enter into the Sacrament with my heart open, honest, and ready to receive what God wanted to pour back into my life. My first meeting with my priest was in early January 2023, and I didn't make my first confession until over two months later, as we were entering the Lenten season that year.

Was I nervous? Absolutely. I put it off once or twice. But ultimately, I used that time to look inward through an examination of conscience and to open my heart to God, asking His forgiveness for what felt like a lifetime of sins. I felt fortunate that over the two months I had been with my parish, I had developed a relationship with my priest, which made it easier. Had it been someone I didn't know, the experience would have felt different. But either way, this was about me coming to God and receiving His mercy, so I set aside the uncomfortable feelings and went forward.

There are numerous helpful resources—such as websites, books, and mobile apps—that offer guidance on Reconciliation. Believe me, I took full advantage of them. When I first began reading about the examination of conscience (which I'll discuss later in this chapter), I also came across the concept of a "general confession." It's not a different sacrament but a particular way of confessing mortal sins from your past when you've been away from the Church for a long time. You're not expected to recall every detail. What matters is taking an honest look at the bigger picture—sins across the years, even decades—and bringing them to God.

In the month leading up to my first confession, I used an app called *Laudate*, a Catholic resource with almost everything: daily readings, prayers, the Order of Mass, and even a guide for

RECONCILIATION

Confession. I found that using an examination of conscience guide helped me prepare for the Sacrament with full honesty about my sins and how I had lived for the past forty years.

In March of that year, I attended a Lenten retreat at a nearby Catholic retreat center, where the priest from my parish was giving one of the talks. While I had no specific plans to go to confession that day, there was a time during the retreat when Father announced he'd be available for confessions while others walked the grounds. In that moment, I knew it was time. It was time to bring God forty years of sins I had been carrying. I had my list and the prayers I needed. My heart was open, but still, I was nervous.

Father set aside a space for private confessions outdoors, on the porch of a small house by the pond. I couldn't imagine a better setting, especially since all my childhood confessions had been inside a booth. I did feel ready, but I also felt a sense of shame and embarrassment. Father eased me in by acknowledging how long it had been and reassuring me that he would guide me through it. I began, "Bless me, Father, for I have sinned. It has been forty years since my last confession." Just saying those words felt monumental. "Forty years" sounded like something out of a movie.

I asked if it was okay to use my phone, where I had saved my list of sins, and Father assured me it was not only okay but encouraged. I also told him I might need some counsel along the way. He said that would be fine. I began with the sins I considered the most serious—the ones that directly violated the commandments. Looking back, I didn't include many venial sins, but I wasn't there yet. I needed to be honest about the more serious ones I had been carrying for all those years.

Father was gentle with me, but he was also direct when it mattered. And that was needed. I've been told I can be an overexplainer, and confession isn't the place for too much backstory. Still, Father gave me space when I needed it.

I went through my list, determined to be as thorough as I could. I came with nine sins written down, and even that felt like a lot for a general confession. What surprised me most was that Father asked a few direct follow-up questions. Not randomly, but about certain sins I had already brought up. I won't go into those here, but it's worth noting: a priest may gently press for clarity, especially if something you mention touches on an area that needs more honesty or healing.

After I finished, Father said reassuringly, "Good, thorough confession." I felt good about that. He asked me to say the Act of Contrition. I hadn't memorized it, but I had it on my phone. And then I heard the words I hadn't heard in decades: "I absolve you from your sins in the name of the Father, and of the Son, and of the Holy Spirit."

And that was it. It was over. I was forgiven for a lifetime of sins. I felt relief. I felt something powerful. I felt God's love.

As for the penance, I was expecting something long and complicated. That's how it felt as a kid, after all. One of the sins I had confessed had to do with honoring our mother and father, and in my case, that meant reflecting on my relationship with my mother. Father simply asked me to pray for her and to pray one decade of the Rosary. There was just one problem—I didn't have a Rosary. When I told him that, he pulled one from his pocket and handed it to me. "You can borrow mine," he said. I told him I'd return it the following week.

As I walked away, I felt happy—truly happy. I was so relieved to have gotten it all out. The weight I'd been carrying was lifted. Even now, I get overwhelmed when I think about how Jesus loves us enough to die for our sins. And how freely He forgives, no matter what we've done or how long we've been away. That's what Reconciliation is about, accepting God's love and mercy.

And that's how it was for me. It wasn't bad at all. Today, I see the Sacrament of Reconciliation as a gift from God, meant to keep us grounded and growing in our faith. God wasn't waiting to punish me. He was waiting to welcome me back to His home. My home. I didn't need perfect words to have a good confession. I just needed honesty.

I share my story because if you're feeling uncertain or even a little scared about going to confession after time away, I want you to know that it's okay. Truly, it is. You don't need perfect words or a perfect memory—just a willing heart. God isn't waiting to shame you. He's waiting to meet you with mercy.

And that's what this sacrament is really about. In the next section, we'll look at how Reconciliation isn't just about confessing what went wrong; it's about being healed, restored, and drawn back into grace.

HOW THE SACRAMENT HEALS AND RESTORES GRACE

When I returned to my Catholic faith and the Sacrament of Reconciliation, it took time to understand how the sacrament truly works. The truth is, we may never fully understand it, but what I can say with confidence is that it's absolutely about God's mercy, healing, and grace. It's not just about getting rid of guilt; it's about being reconnected to God's life within us, to His presence, and His Church. That grace isn't just a feeling; it's God's life poured back into us. It strengthens us, heals us, and restores the damage that sin has caused, even when we can't see or feel it right away. Reconciliation isn't just an abstract concept or a piece of Church theology. It's a living sacrament, essential to Catholic life, and especially important for those returning to the Catholic faith.

What is grace? While the word "grace" is used across all Christian faiths, it seems to carry more layers within Catholic teaching. Many people think of grace simply as God's favor, and that's true. But for Catholics, grace is more than that. It's God's presence within us. Grace helps us better understand His love, become more faithful disciples, and make good choices in our daily lives, even when it is difficult. For me, it's those moments of clarity when I see God, myself, and the world around me more truthfully.

The Church teaches us the difference between sanctifying grace and actual grace. *Sanctifying grace* is the steady, ongoing gift that makes us holy and keeps us in a state of friendship with God. It's what we receive at our Baptism, and what is restored through Reconciliation when we've lost it through mortal sin. *Actual grace* is different, though just as important. It is God's help in the moment, giving us the strength to do what's right when it's hard, to turn away from sin, or to follow His will in a particular situation. Both are important, and both show how deeply God desires to stay close to us and help us grow. Grace doesn't always come with emotion. For some, it might feel like peace. For others, strength. I tend to experience it as clarity—that's when I recognize grace at work.

Sin isn't just bad behavior on our part. It wounds our relationship with God. When we commit a mortal sin, we break our communion with Him. The grace we discussed earlier, God's life within us, is severed. But when we go to Confession, after an honest and thorough examination of conscience, and receive absolution from the priest, that grace is restored. Simply put, it opens the door again, allowing us to live in friendship with God. It wasn't until I came back to the Church that I began to understand, through the reading and reflection that now shapes this book.

There's healing that happens through this sacrament. Sin damages the part of us that was made to be close to God. Mortal sin cuts us off entirely, and even venial sin can gradually weaken our desire for Him. I've heard Reconciliation described as a kind of spiritual field hospital. In the middle of the battle, when we're bruised and worn down by sin, the sacrament acts like surgery. It heals our wounds and gives us the strength to return to the fight.

As I mentioned earlier, after my first confession, I felt a great sense of relief, as if a heavy weight had been lifted. That confession was focused on the mortal sins I had carried for decades. It was emotional, yes, but also filled with joy. Because I knew that grace had been restored. I knew I had been brought back into communion with God. And from that moment on, I could begin to see more clearly how much He loved me and how to follow Him more faithfully. These days, I focus more on looking inward, paying attention to the virtues and the places where I still need to grow. Do I still struggle with sin? I do. But I also know that the Church has given us this beautiful sacrament to help heal what's broken and restore our relationship with Christ.

But let me be clear: not everyone walks away from confession with an immediate sense of change. You may not feel anything at all. That's okay. Grace is still at work. God is still moving. His healing often happens quietly, beneath the surface, in ways we don't always recognize right away. Even if your heart feels silent or unchanged, trust that something real is taking place. The more often we return to the sacrament, the more clearly we begin to see the work He's doing in us. It doesn't happen all at once but unfolds over time in small and meaningful ways.

Reconciliation isn't just about being forgiven. It's about being drawn back into relationship with God—a relationship that's personal, ongoing, and rooted in love. This sacrament brings real healing. It restores the grace we've lost and renews our connection to the Church and Christ himself. As our understanding deepens, we begin to see Reconciliation for what it truly is—not just a requirement, but a return, a quiet and powerful way of coming home.

PREPARING FOR CONFESSION

Now that we've talked about what Reconciliation is and how it works, it's time to look at how to prepare for your first confession after time away. I want to pause here and acknowledge something important. This step can feel intimidating. That's a normal response—especially if, like me, it's been many years since you last went to confession.

When I first sat down to reflect on my sins, I wasn't sure where to begin. I recall feeling overwhelmed and a bit uncertain about myself. If you're feeling that way, too, I want you to know it's okay. Whatever you're feeling right now, whether it's uncertainty, anxiety, or even fear, it's part of the process. It's God beginning to stir your heart as He draws you back. So, try to set aside any pressure to get everything perfect. Reconciliation isn't about ticking boxes or following all the steps just right. It's not about punishment. It's about mercy, healing, and the love of God, who's calling you back.

Finding confession times at your parish or in your area should be pretty straightforward, depending on the size of the church and your priest's schedule. Start with your parish website or bulletin, or check the website of the church you plan to visit. You can also call the church office directly. Confession doesn't have to be at your home parish. You can go to any Catholic church with any priest. Many churches also offer extended confession times during Lent and Advent, so be sure to check. If it's your first confession in many years and you're feeling especially nervous or unsure, consider calling the parish to see if the priest might be available to meet with you outside of the regular confession schedule. Sometimes, having a little extra time and space makes it easier to settle your heart and speak freely.

Doing an examination of conscience is one of the most critical steps in preparing for confession. The Church encourages us to reflect honestly on our lives and sins, guided by Scripture. The Ten Commandments and the Beatitudes are both powerful starting points.

To be honest, I hadn't thought about using the Beatitudes to prepare for confession until I began reading and researching for this book. But the more I sat with them, the more I realized how helpful they are, especially for someone returning to the sacrament. Instead of just focusing on what you've done wrong, the Beatitudes invite us to reflect on the kind of life Jesus calls us to live: humble, compassionate, merciful, just, and peace-seeking.

I've also found that using a trusted examination of conscience guide or app is a helpful way to reflect on my sins. There are many versions available for both adults and teens. A quick search in your phone's app store will bring up several reliable options.

Try to do your examination of conscience in prayerful reflection. You don't need to finish it all at once. Spreading it out over several days may be better. I began doing mine in the mornings alongside prayer, then later during Adoration. Do what helps you listen to yourself and the Holy Spirit. The point isn't to be perfect. It's to be honest.

Once you've had time to reflect, the next step to think about is contrition. Contrition is a genuine sorrow for your sins and a desire to turn back to God. I remember feeling unsure about what "contrition" really meant. Was I sorry enough? Were the feelings

RECONCILIATION

I had the right ones? Over time, I came to see it more simply as a sincere desire to reconnect with God and live differently.

The Church teaches that there are two types of contrition: *perfect* and *imperfect*. Perfect contrition means being sorry for your sins because you love God and regret having hurt Him. It's not about fear or guilt—it's about love.

Imperfect contrition means being sorry because of the consequences your sins may bring, or because you recognize how they've hurt others. That kind of sorrow is still real. And when you bring it into the Sacrament of Reconciliation, it is enough. God meets that imperfect sorrow with mercy.

Let's now walk through what happens during confession. For some, it may have only been a few years, and you'll likely remember the steps. But if it's been decades, like it was for me, knowing what to expect can bring some peace. However, remember that the priest is there to help guide you if you're unsure about what to do.

Some churches, especially older or larger ones, still have a traditional confessional where you can kneel behind a screen and remain anonymous. Others may offer face-to-face confession in a quiet room or a chapel space. Both are entirely valid. If you're feeling nervous and the anonymous option is available, it might help you feel more at ease. The important thing is simply showing up with a desire to make a good confession.

Start by greeting the priest. If others are waiting, keep it brief. Then say, "Bless me, Father, for I have sinned," and tell him how long it's been since your last confession. An estimate is fine.

You can say a short prayer before you begin. I often ask God for courage and honesty as I prepare to speak. It helps settle my heart and focus my intention.

Then confess your sins, one by one. It may be helpful to name the sin using the Church's language. For example: "I have committed the sin of pride," or "I've fallen into the sin of anger." If necessary, specify how often it occurred. You don't need to explain or tell stories. Just keep things clear and direct. If the priest needs more details, he'll ask, as he wants you to make a good confession.

You don't have to remember everything, just do your best. If you forget something and remember it later, especially a venial sin, bring it up in your next confession. If it's a mortal sin, return to confession as soon as you can.

After you finish, the priest will give you your penance. It's usually a prayer or action he asks you to do after confession. It's not a punishment—it's a response. It might be to pray a decade of the Rosary, a Scripture reading, or an act of kindness. Try to complete it soon, while the experience is still fresh in your mind.

The priest may also offer brief counsel. Listen, and feel free to ask clarifying questions. Be mindful of others who may be waiting.

Next, you'll pray the Act of Contrition. This is a prayer of sorrow and a promise to try again. If you don't have it memorized, it's fine to read it. Here's a common version:

> *Act of Contrition*
> My God, I am sorry for my sins with all my heart.
> In choosing to do wrong and failing to do good,
> I have sinned against You,
> whom I should love above all things.
> I firmly intend, with Your help, to do penance,
> to sin no more, and to avoid whatever leads me to sin.
> Our Savior Jesus Christ suffered and died for us.
> In His name, my God, have mercy. Amen.

Note: This is one of several versions of the Act of Contrition approved by the Catholic Church. You may use any version that expresses sincere sorrow and the desire to return to God.

The priest will then say the words of absolution. You'll make the sign of the cross and receive forgiveness. Say "thank you," and you're done. Just remember to do your penance as soon as possible.

Many priests are okay with you bringing written notes or using your phone. Just ask. I keep my list of sins and prayers on my phone and delete them after confession.

One common fear people have is whether the priest will repeat what they say. Please know this—he cannot. The Seal of Confession means the priest can never repeat anything you say, not to anyone, not for any reason. The Church teaches that this seal is absolute; no circumstance, no pressure, and no authority can ever compel a priest to break it. Even if threatened with prison or death, he is bound to silence. That is how sacred this trust is. You can speak freely and safely.

Finally, remember that Reconciliation isn't a test or a performance. It's a conversation with God, one that takes place through the priest. This is how Jesus gave us the sacrament. It's one more way we turn our hearts back to Him.

THE POWER OF FORGIVENESS

As we explored earlier, the Sacrament of Reconciliation isn't just about removing sin—it's about receiving God's mercy and forgiveness. But it also gives something back to us: peace, freedom, clarity, and the spiritual strength to live as Jesus calls us to. This kind of mercy can restore what we thought was lost. Confession is where the weight lifts, where we find the courage to begin again. It's where we stop carrying everything alone. With that renewed freedom, we can move forward with more honesty, living each day with a sincere desire to follow Christ.

I shared the story of my first confession after being away from the Church for many years, but what I didn't share earlier is how the sacrament helped me forgive myself. I began to let go of the shame that had built up over time and started to see myself not just as someone who had sinned, but as someone who belonged to God. That shift didn't happen overnight. It began with that first confession, and over time, I came to believe that I could truly move forward as a son of God. Self-forgiveness can be hard, especially when sin becomes tangled with our identity or when we have regrets. But remember, you don't have to keep punishing yourself. After you receive forgiveness from the Lord, you can let go. Once we are absolved, Jesus doesn't hold on to our sins, and neither should we.

Not all wounds we bring to the sacrament come from things we've done. Sometimes they come from what others have done to us, or from experiences that may have damaged our trust in others. During my first confession, I shared something from my childhood—not anything like abuse, but rather some difficult dynamics from how I was raised that I'd been carrying for years. I remember Father gently reminding me that confession is a place to name our own sins, not the sins of others. But he also assured me it was okay to bring those emotions into the conversation. Feelings like anger, betrayal, or confusion don't need to be hidden. The priest can't "fix" what happened, but naming those emotions in the presence of Christ can be a first step toward healing.

The Church asks practicing Catholics to go to confession at least once a year, especially if they're aware of mortal sin. But even when we aren't carrying mortal sin, the Church encourages more frequent confession. It's not just about serious failings; it's a chance to grow spiritually and work through the ordinary struggles that pull us away from God. Since returning to the Church, I've tried to maintain a rhythm of going every 60 to 90 days. I mark it on my calendar and make a point to go before Lent and Advent as well. I find that regular confession helps me work on virtues and address areas for improvement. It reminds me that even venial sins, left unchecked, can gradually weaken our desire to stay close to Christ.

Recent polling I've seen indicates that about 42 percent of U.S. Catholics go to confession at least once a year, while 24 percent go less than once a year, and 18 percent never go. The encouraging news is that the number of Catholics who go monthly has grown from 10 percent in 2022 to 16 percent in 2024. That percentage includes everyone, from those who attend weekly to those who attend even more frequently.

So why do some Catholics go so often? I used to wonder that myself. At first, even monthly confession seemed like a lot. Then I learned that Pope John Paul II went to confession every week, sometimes more. That amazed me, but it also helped me understand that regular confession isn't necessarily about major sins. It's about staying rooted in grace. It's about recognizing how things like pride, impatience, distraction, and judgment can take hold in our lives, and learning to open our hearts to God again and again.

Reconciliation

You don't have to start there. But as you return to the Church and begin to trust more in God, you may find yourself drawn to the sacrament more often. And when that happens, you'll understand why it means so much to so many people.

The Sacrament of Reconciliation is truly a gift. If you've been thinking about going, just go. You don't need perfect words—just an open heart. Confession is where God's mercy meets our honesty. It's where something new can begin, where healing starts, and where the road home becomes real.

5

Finding Your Place in the Parish
A Time of Renewal

COMING BACK TO THE Church carried deep meaning for me. But it also brought questions—some practical, others more personal. For both Mary Beth and me, there was a lot to sort through. I realized pretty quickly that finding my place again meant more than just showing up for Mass or joining a Bible study. We were building new relationships, facing new realities, and revisiting things we thought were settled.

For many returning Catholics, one of the first things that needs attention is marriage and how that marriage aligns with the Catholic faith. That was certainly true for me. I never expected to have to examine our 33-year marriage, but that's where my return to the Church and parish life began.

This chapter is about that kind of renewal. Not just in your marriage, but in your sense of belonging and purpose as you step back into the life of the Church. At some point, you stop feeling like a visitor in the pew. You realize you're not just attending—you're home.

WHEN COMING HOME MEANS REVISITING YOUR MARRIAGE

Returning to the Church remains one of the greatest gifts of my life. But three years ago, when I first returned, I didn't fully understand all the questions that would begin to surface for us. As I started receiving the sacraments again, one of the first things we had to face was a question about our marriage.

I want to be clear from the start—I'm not an expert on Church teaching, and this section doesn't offer official advice. But I've lived through one of the more common marriage situations. Since then, I've spoken with others who've faced different and even more difficult questions about marriage and returning to the faith. What I can tell you is this: you aren't alone, there is support, and there's always a path forward.

I've learned that while every situation is unique, Catholics remain bound by canon law in marriage. For a marriage to be valid in the eyes of the Church, it must be witnessed by a priest, deacon, or bishop who has been properly delegated by Church authority, with two witnesses present. Canon law also requires that both spouses give their full and free consent to the marriage. Simply having a priest present isn't enough; he must be officially authorized to witness the marriage.

As you begin to settle into parish life, you may find there are things to sort through. There may be aspects of your marriage that need to be addressed so you (and possibly your spouse) can come into full communion with the Church. What I've come to appreciate is that the Church doesn't just give you a checklist. It walks with you. There are people who will help you understand what needs to happen and guide you through the process gently.

I mentioned in an earlier chapter that our 33-year marriage had to undergo the process of convalidation. Convalidation is the Church's way of making a civil or non-Catholic marriage valid in the eyes of the Church, usually by having the couple exchange vows again in the presence of a priest or deacon and two witnesses. If both spouses are baptized, the marriage also becomes sacramental.

When I returned to my Catholic faith in 2023, and Mary Beth began her path toward conversion, neither of us knew what that would involve. We had to answer questions, provide affidavits from family and friends, and go through the convalidation process to bring our marriage into full communion with the Church.

That conversation wasn't easy at first. It felt like the Church was asking us to prove that our marriage was real. That was painful. But after several meetings with our priest, we began to understand what the Church was really saying. Convalidation didn't mean our life together hadn't been real or meaningful because it most certainly had. But bringing it into the Church gave it a sacramental grace we didn't realize we were missing. For us, it was a simple but meaningful step. It brought clarity, peace, and a renewed sense of commitment. Every situation is different and often complex, but the process can lead to deeper peace and a greater understanding of purpose in your marriage.

For many Catholics returning after years away, marriage questions are among the first to come up. Below are five of the most common situations returning Catholics may face:

Married Outside the Church (No Prior Marriages)

Suppose you were married in a civil ceremony or a non-Catholic church, and neither you nor your spouse had a prior marriage. In that case, a convalidation is usually required to bring your marriage into full communion with the Church. However, if a Catholic priest or deacon was present *with proper delegation from the diocese*, a convalidation may not be needed. Your priest or deacon can help confirm the details.

Divorced and Remarried (Without an Annulment)

This is one of the more difficult situations. If a Catholic divorces and remarries without an annulment of the first marriage, the Church views the new union as "irregular." In this case, the person is generally not able to receive the sacraments until the situation is resolved. That resolution usually involves petitioning the Church for an annulment of the prior marriage. If granted, the current marriage can then go through convalidation. Your priest or deacon can walk you through the steps.

Divorced, Not Remarried

If you're divorced but have not remarried or entered into a romantic relationship, you can return to the sacraments. An annulment is not required unless you plan to remarry in the Church. Making a good confession is always a wise first step. The Church also offers support for the emotional and spiritual healing that comes after divorce. You don't have to walk that road alone.

Married to a Non-Catholic Christian

This is more common than many realize. When a Catholic marries a baptized Christian from another faith tradition, it's considered a "mixed marriage" and requires permission from the Church. If the person is unbaptized, a dispensation (another form of approval) is required. In both cases, the Catholic spouse must promise to continue as a practicing Catholic and to raise any children in the Catholic faith. A priest or deacon can still bless the marriage later (such as on an anniversary), but a blessing does not make an invalid marriage valid. Only convalidation, through a new exchange of consent before the Church, can do that.

One Spouse Returning, the Other Not Interested (Yet)

This is another common scenario and often one of the hardest. It can feel lonely when one spouse is coming home to the Church while the other, Catholic or not, wants no part of it. If the marriage is valid in the eyes of the Church, the returning spouse can participate fully in the sacraments, even if their partner doesn't attend Mass or share the faith. The non-interested spouse doesn't need to convert or attend Mass for the returning Catholic to come home. If the marriage is *not* considered valid, a convalidation may be required.

There are many other marriage situations, and some are more complicated, but these are the most common, to my knowledge. It's important to know that you aren't alone and you don't have to navigate this without support. I encourage you to meet with your priest or deacon and be honest about your circumstances. The more clearly you can share the details, the easier it will be for the Church to help you move forward. The Church has walked with many people through similar experiences and has a process in place to help. And it's not just about checking a box or completing a formality. That was the mistake Mary Beth and I made early on; we thought convalidation was just an administrative step. It wasn't. It became one of the most meaningful steps in our lives together.

So, as you step more fully into parish life, remember that God meets you where you are: in your marriage, in your home, and in your heart. This journey is about healing, wholeness, and the gift of grace. Let it unfold in God's time.

RETURNING—AND FEELING OUT OF PLACE

Finding a Catholic parish in my hometown became one of the most important parts of my return to the Church. As I mentioned earlier, I'm naturally an introvert. Meeting new people doesn't come easily to me, and I've never been one to jump into social settings without hesitation. But something had shifted. Even Mary Beth noticed it. It wasn't just that I wanted to go to Mass—I wanted to belong. I felt drawn not only to return but to participate. To serve. For the first time in a long while, I had both the desire and the time to offer something back. I was mostly retired by then, and I sensed that God was opening a door for me.

Still, those early steps weren't smooth or simple. Wanting to be part of a parish is one thing. Figuring out how to do that after years away from church is something else entirely.

Finding Your Place in the Parish

There's a certain awkwardness that can come with returning to Mass, which I've already talked about, but settling into a new parish brings its own set of challenges. For me, I didn't just feel new to this particular church. I felt new to the whole idea of parish life. I had a strong sense of spiritual urgency about returning to the Church and reconnecting with a Catholic community, and that urgency sometimes made things more complicated. If you're feeling unsure, unsettled, or even a little out of place, those feelings are completely normal.

One thing that helped me early on was how much this parish reminded me of the one I grew up in back in South Carolina. That familiarity made it easier to settle in. There was something comforting about the size, the atmosphere, even the way people greeted one another. Those early visits in 2023 brought some uncertainty, but the kindness of the people around us helped ease that right away. Did it still feel awkward at times? Absolutely. I think it was easier for Mary Beth; fellowship had always been an important part of church life when we attended the Methodist church. For me, not so much. In my first conversation with our priest, I even said, "Church is about me and Jesus." That's where I was at the time. Looking back, I can now see just how central parish life would become for me. The friends in faith I've come to know have been a significant part of my journey, and in some ways, an inspiration for this book.

I touched on this in chapter 3, but on one of the first Sundays we attended, something small yet important happened. After the final blessing, as we gathered our things, someone came up to Mary Beth and me and invited us to the adult education class that was happening right after Mass. It was a simple and sincere invitation. But it caught me off guard.

In the past, I would have said no, especially that early on. Saying yes to something like that just wasn't natural for me. And to this day, Mary Beth still laughs and says she couldn't believe I agreed to go. But I did. And looking back, I think it was the Holy Spirit prompting me to step forward. That one moment opened a door. The man who invited us, and his wife, are now two of our dearest friends in the parish.

It goes back to something I said earlier—if someone invites you to a church event or gathering, consider it more than a casual ask. It might be the Holy Spirit at work. Say yes, even if it feels a little uncomfortable. You never know what, or who, God may be placing in your path.

Some people worry that they'll be judged when they return to the Church. I understand that. I had a few of those thoughts myself. I remember wondering if people were sizing me up, curious about why I had left or whether I truly belonged. But in the end, that fear was just in my head. No one ever made me feel that way. I've since met others who were also returning after many years, and their experiences have been similar. Most people are simply glad you're there. And you don't have to explain yourself right away. You can share your story at your own pace, or not at all if you aren't comfortable. Just being there is enough.

If you're newly returning and beginning to feel more confident in your decision, take some small steps forward. Sit in the back if that's more comfortable. Stay a few minutes after Mass to pray. Say hello to someone nearby. Ask a question. Offer a smile. These small actions begin to open the door toward something deeper. You don't have to know what's next. Just be present.

About a month after we joined our new parish, I knew I wanted to do more than just attend Mass on Sundays. Mary Beth felt the same way. We were both ready for more. But I also knew I needed to be careful. It's easy to jump in too fast, especially when you're excited, and that can lead to frustration, for you and sometimes for others. You might step into something that someone else has been quietly taking care of for a long time—something they genuinely enjoy doing. I've learned that wanting to help is good, but it's just as important to listen, observe, and ease your way in. In time, the right opportunities will come, and they'll come with peace, not pressure. There's a certain grace in taking your time.

GETTING INVOLVED AT YOUR OWN PACE

After forty years away, I returned with a deep sense of urgency. I felt like I was making up for lost time, and that motivated me to give back, not just through tithing, but also by volunteering wherever I could. I had the flexibility, the motivation, and a strong sense that God was calling me to act. So I jumped right in. I didn't know where I belonged, so I tried to belong everywhere.

I figured if God had waited forty years for me, the least I could do was show up wherever I was needed. I was excited. I wanted to help. And I wanted to be helpful to a Church that had welcomed me back so generously. Looking back, I can see how that might have come on a little strong, especially to those who had been part of the parish for many years. It's just how I tend to approach things, especially when I feel called. I genuinely felt pulled to step forward, as if God was urging me on.

Even so, not one person made us feel like outsiders. They simply made room. We were lucky in that sense, welcomed from the start. No one ever made us feel out of place. That kind of grace and hospitality isn't something I take for granted.

I never had anyone pull me aside and tell me to slow down. The message came more quietly than that. During a particularly hectic week—I think we had five different church activities—I found myself sitting in the parish before Mass, completely spent. And in that moment, I heard it clearly—"Be still." Not "do more." Just "be still." It was simple, but it reached me. And it was exactly what I needed in that moment. Sometimes, God has to wear us out before we'll listen.

Looking back now, I want to tell anyone coming home to the Church what I wish someone had told me: slow down. You've already made the hardest step by walking through those doors. There's no rush to find your place. You don't have to prove your faith by doing everything at once or attending daily Mass to show that you're serious. Simply show up, breathe, and let God reveal where you're needed. He will. He always does.

While I don't have any regrets about how I came back to the Church, I do sometimes think I moved a little too quickly in a few areas. About six months after returning, I was approached by the only altar server we had at the time. He was serving alone, with no youth servers and no one else to rotate with. He asked if I might consider learning to serve at the altar, as he hoped to occasionally sit in the pews with his wife. At first, it was just a casual conversation. But a few weeks later, I went back to him and said, "Let's do it. Train me."

I felt called to serve, not just to help our priest, but to be closer to the Eucharist. To this day, serving at the altar with our priest is one of the great joys in my spiritual life. But even as I said yes, part of me wondered if I was moving too fast. I had only been back in the Church for six months, and there was still a lot I didn't know. I had so much to relearn. I don't regret saying yes, and I'd recommend it to anyone. However, I've come to realize that some roles in the Church require more background than I initially thought. Enthusiasm without context can create awkward moments for you and others. In my case, it worked out. However, for most people, especially in the early stages, it may be too much too soon.

That's why I think it helps to start small. In most parishes, there's someone who helps coordinate volunteers and ministries. In smaller churches, it might be a lay leader or a small core group. In larger parishes, it could be someone on staff, such as a ministry coordinator, a parish office contact, or a director of parish life.

Either way, look for low-pressure ways to get involved. Attend a Bible study or a formation group. Say yes to a single event, like helping at a parish meal. Or offer behind-the-scenes help—set-up, clean-up, hospitality. Those kinds of things matter more than people realize.

As with any church, there are always things that need to be fixed or maintained. If something falls within your skill set, offer to help, but first find out how it has been handled in the past. You may not realize that someone's already been faithfully taking care of that task for years. Around the church, we all have our little ministries, and they often mean more to us than others can see.

Even when a role appears to need attention, someone may already take pride in doing it. Offer to help someone, not replace them. And if you're unsure, just ask. "Is there someone already doing this?" You don't have to lead to be involved.

It also helps to learn the culture of your particular parish. Every church is different, and so are its people. That's a good thing, but it means taking the time to understand how things work. Learn the history. Watch how decisions are made. Notice who's already doing what, and what they seem to care about. Don't assume that all roles are up for grabs, or that something that looks disorganized is being ignored. Sometimes, things aren't broken; they're just running on history, tradition, or the silent work of someone behind the scenes. Respect what's already happening, especially when it's coming from long-time parishioners.

There's no deadline for finding your place in the parish. For me, it took almost a full year before things began to feel natural. So take your time. Let it unfold. A simple prayer can help: "Lord, just show me where I'm needed." Your worth isn't tied to how involved you are. You've already been called home. And that, by itself, is more than enough.

BUILDING A FAITH COMMUNITY

Much of this chapter has focused on getting involved in parish life, and I can't overstate how important that is when you're finding your way back to the Catholic faith. A parish grounds us. It gives us a spiritual home. But for many of us, especially those coming back after years away, we also need something more. We need connection, support, and opportunities to keep learning. We need a faith community that helps us not just attend church, but live out our faith in daily life. That's what this section is about—how to build a wider circle of faith-filled relationships that can walk with you, challenge you, and help you grow, not just now, but for the long road ahead.

Building a larger faith community is important because, as we grow in faith and navigate different seasons of life, our needs and priorities can evolve. It is helpful to maintain a broad perspective on the Church, its people, and its teachings. This is especially true as you learn to live your faith more intentionally, every day.

In my own experience, and conversations with others, I've come to believe that returning to the Church can sometimes feel surprisingly isolating. That loneliness can happen for all kinds of reasons—maybe old friends have drifted away, or perhaps you're simply in a different place in life. I felt it, especially early on, because for the first time in decades, I was prioritizing God and my faith. That shift was hard for some family and friends to understand. But I was also fortunate. Mary Beth was walking that road with me, learning the Catholic faith for the first time after a lifetime as a Protestant. In many ways, that gave me permission to approach things as a beginner too, and I found that to be comforting.

This kind of isolation may not be universal, but it's real. And it's more likely to happen if you don't get involved at the local level. That's why it's important to push past your comfort zone and begin building friendships within the faith. If you're feeling a little alone in the process, that doesn't mean your return is failing. It may just mean your heart is craving a more grounded sense of belonging as you draw closer to God.

Still, the parish alone may not always be enough, especially for someone returning to the Church with renewed energy and a desire to deepen their faith. For many of us, the spiritual and relational needs can feel stronger than before. That was certainly true for me. Beyond attending Mass on Sundays and weekdays, I found that building a broader faith community supported my return. It complemented the structure of parish life and gave me a stronger foundation as I relearned what it means to live as a Catholic.

Those relationships often begin small. But consistency is what matters. You don't have to find the perfect group or friendship right away. Just show up where it feels meaningful and keep returning. That might mean joining a parish Bible study or attending one hosted by another parish in your diocese. Men's and women's groups can be especially meaningful, particularly when they bring people together from different parishes. A Rosary or

Adoration group may feel intimidating at first, but it often leads to a deeper relationship with Christ and lasting bonds with others who are walking the same path.

When I first returned to the Church, our priest encouraged everyone in RCIA to attend Adoration. I started going a couple of times a month. Over time, I began to notice something unexpected. Many of the same people were there each time—fellow parishioners, some of whom I already knew. But sharing that holy space created a different kind of connection. There's a quiet power in kneeling in prayer beside someone you see each week. It has become one of the most meaningful parts of how I've built community.

The Catholic community doesn't begin and end with Sunday Mass or your home church. One of the beautiful things about the faith is that it's both local and global, deeply rooted and consistent no matter where you go. When Mary Beth and I travel, whether across the U.S. or abroad, one of our great joys is attending Mass in a new church, even when the language is unfamiliar. As a returning Catholic, it helps to remember that your spiritual life can be enriched by connecting with the wider Church beyond your parish.

Every diocese offers events, resources, and opportunities for learning and service. Check in periodically with your diocesan website or newsletter. You might discover a speaker series, a day of reflection, or a retreat that offers just what you need, often closer to home than you'd expect.

There are also Catholic organizations that can support your journey, depending on your interests and needs. Groups like the Knights of Columbus or local women's ministries can offer a sense of purpose and belonging. And with so many online forums, study groups, and virtual communities now available, you don't have to be limited by geography. Don't overlook retreats either. Some of the most important moments in my own return came from stepping away for a weekend to pray, reflect, and listen. In the Archdiocese of Atlanta, where I live, I've found plenty of retreat options within a short drive. See what your diocese might offer. You may come across an opportunity that helps you take the next step.

New friendships and mentorship opportunities may take time to develop. Over the past several years, I've made new friends both within and beyond my church community. I've come to value the wisdom of lifelong Catholics who have stayed faithful through every season, through joys, struggles, Church scandals, and leadership changes. There is something to be learned from that kind of perseverance.

In my case, I've also been blessed with a strong connection to our priest and deacon. They were among the first people I spoke with when returning, and over time, they've become trusted mentors. These relationships can grow naturally. There's no need to force anything, but be open. Sometimes, a simple hello after Mass or a casual conversation at a retreat can lead to something more meaningful.

I want to leave you with a word of encouragement—be generous and open. That may sound simple, but it can be surprisingly difficult, especially when you're just coming back. This was one of the hardest parts for me. Being willing to show up, to say yes to an invitation, to speak first, or to offer your gifts and time to the Church takes courage. Every one of these choices matters. But I've learned that service often opens the door to something more meaningful. Building community isn't just about what you receive. It's also about how you show up for others who are on the same path.

As we come back to the Church, building a faith community may take time. And it should. It's worth the effort. You don't need hundreds of people. Just a small handful of companions who can walk with you, challenge you, and pray with you as you grow in your relationship with God. Return to this simple prayer: "God, please help me find my people—the ones you've chosen to walk with me." In time, those relationships won't just support you, they'll invite you to give something back.

SERVING WITH HUMILITY AND PURPOSE

When I started to settle into a routine in parish life, I realized that *how* and *when* we begin serving is only part of the picture. The deeper question is why we serve. That's what this section is about. In an earlier part of this chapter, I discussed easing your way in by talking with others, observing what's already happening, asking questions, and finding a sustainable pace. But once that's in place, another layer begins to emerge, the desire to serve with real purpose and intention. Not just to stay busy. Not to prove something to yourself or others. This is the stage of discernment, where you begin to offer yourself in ways that reflect both your gifts and the humility Christ modeled for us. That can be challenging at times, especially in a busy, active parish. But this is where the heart of service begins to take shape. And it's often where a renewed Catholic faith starts to deepen.

So, the question at this point isn't *"How can I help?"* but rather, *"Why am I helping?"* That kind of spiritual discernment is foundational as you begin serving in your parish or the wider Catholic community. It doesn't mean overthinking. It means listening, asking God to show you where and how He wants you to serve. It means being honest with yourself and staying open to where your gifts might be needed most.

Many returning Catholics, including myself, feel a pull to jump in right away. That's perfectly fine. At first, we might feel uncertain about how to align that service with a deeper purpose. But that clarity tends to come with time. Reflecting on humility can help clarify things. Humility grounds us. It reminds us that we're not serving to be seen or to earn God's favor. We're serving out of love. It shifts our focus from outcome to intention. It helps us say yes for the right reasons and no without guilt. When humility leads, we're more likely to serve in ways that are sustainable, sincere, and rooted in prayer. That's what keeps service from becoming just another obligation and allows it to become a source of grace.

My long career in state government gave me experience in leadership, organization, and follow-through. When I considered how to serve in my own parish and the broader Catholic community, those were the areas I naturally leaned toward. I try to offer those strengths where they're needed most, especially in support of the priorities our priest identifies.

But serving at the altar was something entirely different. I had been approached about getting trained, including helping in the sacristy and caring for the sacred vessels after Mass. At first, I wasn't sure. So I prayed about it. I spent time in quiet reflection, just trying to be open. What came back to me again and again was the Eucharist. I felt drawn to it in a new way. I wasn't looking for a role or a title. I just wanted to be closer to the heart of the Church, to the source of what I had come back to. Over time, it became clear that this was one way I could serve, with humility, reverence, and purpose.

There can also be an internal pressure to do more. I experience this from time to time, and I've noticed it in others as well. That's usually when I have to pause and ask myself what's really driving me. Maybe it's the feeling of wanting to make up for lost time, which is something I wrestle with, having been away from the Church for so long. Or maybe it's a need to prove that my return is real. But I remind myself often—my worth isn't tied to how much I do at church. I think this is something many of us face, especially those coming back later in life. When my motivation slips into wanting to be seen or simply staying busy, it usually leaves me feeling drained instead of fulfilled.

There will also come a time when you need to say no to something. I once read that saying no can be the holiest thing to do. This is about setting healthy boundaries and recognizing that you can't say yes to everything. Saying no gives you more space to focus on your own gifts, and it opens the door for others to step in. I've had to remind myself repeatedly that sometimes God calls me to simply be still. I'm a natural doer, so that's not always easy. I've been known to overcommit, not just in church but in life, and I'm slowly learning how to find peace in saying no.

I often think of the way we serve as our quiet little missions, the things we do when no one's looking. These are often the most fruitful acts of all. Simple things like unlocking the church early, restocking coffee supplies for Bible study, praying privately for someone, or encouraging a friend after Mass. They don't draw attention, but they strengthen the Church in lasting ways.

This kind of hidden ministry is where humility truly takes root. You're not serving to impress. You're simply offering what you have with sincerity and consistency. And often, it's the ongoing acts of love that matter most. Showing up to pray. Being dependable in a small role and offering encouragement behind the scenes. These small acts not only help others but shape who we're becoming.

It helps me to remember that service isn't about being noticed. It's really about growing in relationship with God. Service can also become an extension of prayer, a lived expression of our ongoing conversation with the Lord. As I've said elsewhere in this book, a short prayer or reflection can help keep your focus where it belongs.

Something like, "Lord, help me always serve for love, not recognition."

When we serve with humility, we not only grow closer to God but also become a steady light for others who may be searching as well. That's how faith extends beyond the church walls, shaping daily life, deepening relationships, and touching the hearts of those still on their way home.

6

Living Out Your Faith
Strengthening Yourself and Reaching Others

RETURNING TO THE CATHOLIC faith can be an emotional and exciting experience, but it can also feel disorienting. The rituals, the language, even the silence of Mass can seem unfamiliar. And as the initial momentum of returning fades, something deeper begins: the slow, steady work of living out faith every day.

This chapter is about that next step. How do we build a relationship with God that's consistent, rooted in daily practice, and sustainable over time? Not just on Sundays or during spiritual highs, but in ordinary routines, quiet mornings, and when we're tired or distracted.

This isn't about mastering religious tasks or checking boxes. It's about learning to stay close to God, especially when things feel difficult or uncertain. It's about finding peace in a noisy, divided world and becoming the kind of person whose steady faith offers light to others, wherever they are in their journey.

But honestly, that sounds bigger than it is. Most of the time, it's just being present.

When we return to the Church, we don't need to have all the answers. But we do need to begin living differently. That might mean learning to pray again, building a space for faith in our homes, or simply asking God for the grace to keep showing up. We say yes to what's right in front of us. His timing, His mercy, and the people He's asking us to love—even when we don't feel ready.

REDISCOVERING CATHOLIC PRACTICES

When I was a kid, Catholic practices didn't mean much to me. I just thought that's what we did. I only noticed the difference when I went to church with friends from other denominations. Returning to the Church later in life brought back those early memories, and this time, they took on a different meaning. It was the practices I had once taken for granted that helped me realize what I'd been missing all those years.

I often think of devotions, prayers, sacramentals, and the sacraments themselves as spiritual anchors that steady us as we move toward eternal salvation. Since *The Long Way Home* is a reversion story and a practical guide, not a devotional manual, I won't go too deep into each one here. What I want to offer instead is a reintroduction for anyone who might be curious, hesitant, or unsure where to begin. My hope isn't that you master these practices overnight, but that you consider trying them as you return to the Church and begin rebuilding a life of faith.

Praying the Rosary has been a centuries-old tradition in the Catholic Church. It begins with the Sign of the Cross, then the Apostles' Creed, the Our Father, three Hail Marys (for faith, hope, and charity), and a Glory Be. From there, it moves through five decades, each made up of an Our Father, ten Hail Marys, and another Glory Be. Many also add the Fatima Prayer after each decade. As you pray, you reflect on key moments in the life of Christ, with the help of His mother, Mary. The twenty mysteries are grouped into four sets of five. It's not just repetition, but a reflective way to walk through the mysteries of our salvation, one prayer at a time.

You can also pray the Rosary with specific intentions in mind, such as for your family, parish, the sick, or the need for peace in the world. Each decade can be offered for something in particular, making the Rosary not only a reflection on Christ's life but also a way of placing your own concerns into God's hands. Many Catholics believe that when we pray the Rosary, we're not praying to Mary but *with her*. Like a mother praying with her children, she intercedes for us and gently directs our attention back to her Son. In this way, the Rosary becomes both personal and communal: our voices joined with Mary's, all directed to Christ.

I've talked a little about *Eucharistic Adoration* in earlier chapters. I didn't grow up attending Adoration, but as a returning Catholic, I've come to appreciate the gift it has become in my life. Adoration places us before the Blessed Sacrament—Christ fully present in the consecrated Host—and gives us the chance to simply be with Him in silence. There's no need to perform or "feel" anything in particular. Just bring your love, your gratitude, or whatever you've got that day. When I'm at Adoration, I spend time in prayer, but I also use that hour to read scripture or occasionally a Catholic devotional or spiritual book.

Sacramentals can be a powerful way to keep reminders of God's presence in our daily lives. Objects like holy water, crucifixes, and medals aren't charms, and they aren't magical, but they are tangible expressions of our Catholic faith. Dipping your fingers in holy water as you enter or leave the church reminds you of your Baptism, calling to mind that you belong to Christ. A crucifix in your home or workspace can serve as a reminder of what Christ has done for you, especially during a busy day. Even wearing a cross or a medal, whether it's the Miraculous Medal, the Saint Benedict Medal, or one of a patron saint, can help bring your attention back to God during moments of stress or doubt. These small practices don't replace faith; they help hold it in place.

The *Catholic liturgical calendar*, often referred to as the Church year, is how the Church marks time in relation to the life of Christ. It moves through seasons such as Advent, Christmas, Lent, Easter, and Ordinary Time, each with its own distinct focus and rhythm. The calendar gives shape to our prayer life, helps us reflect on key moments in our faith, and reminds us that we're part of something much bigger than our busy schedules. You'll also notice the Church uses different colors during each season to reflect what we're preparing for or celebrating. These may be seen in the priest's and deacon's vestments, altar cloths, tabernacle and chalice veils, and sometimes even in seasonal decorations.

But we can also live the liturgical year at home. Lighting an Advent wreath, using seasonal colors, abstaining from meat on Fridays during Lent, or celebrating your patron saint's feast day with a special dessert are simple ways to bring the Church year into your daily life.

Creating a *special prayer space* at home can help build a strong habit of prayer in your daily life. It doesn't have to be elaborate—maybe just a comfortable chair by a window or a quiet corner in your home. It could be a place to keep your Bible and other devotionals, and it can serve as your "meeting place" with God. Use it for morning prayer, scripture readings, or evening reflection if that's part of your regular routine. What matters isn't how it looks; it's that you return to it consistently.

I have two spaces in my own home, and the one I choose usually depends on where Mary Beth is. I like to read the daily scriptures and pray after breakfast in the kitchen, but if she's in there, I'll move to my desk in the home office. Having one dedicated space is helpful, but sometimes you just have to be flexible.

I don't have a *home altar*, but I'm curious about the way others use them. Just like a prayer space, a home altar can be a visible reminder that faith belongs in your daily life. You can keep it simple, such as a small table with a crucifix, candle, icon, or a few prayer cards. Some families change theirs with the seasons of the liturgical year. And while a personal prayer corner is usually just for you, a home altar can be something your whole family gathers around.

As you discover ways to live your Catholic faith in daily life, remember you don't have to take on everything at once. Just begin with one or two small practices that help you slow down and stay close to Christ. Maybe it's placing a crucifix in your home, lighting a candle before dinner, or praying a decade of the Rosary before bed. These small choices create space for grace to grow. Over time, they become habits that shape not just what you do, but who you're becoming—someone rooted in faith, even in the middle of ordinary life.

STRENGTHENING YOUR RELATIONSHIP WITH GOD

Earlier, I mentioned the momentum many people feel when they return to the Catholic faith. At first, everything feels new and alive. Prayer comes easily. You look forward to Mass, and you may even attend daily Mass during the week. You join a Bible study, help out around the parish, and say yes to everything. There's a natural energy to it all. A kind of energy that makes full engagement feel almost effortless.

But that emotional momentum doesn't last forever. And that's okay. This is often where something deeper begins to take root—not just belief, but a relationship built on consistency and trust. I don't think God is looking for performance. I believe He's looking for presence. Especially in the moments when being present is difficult.

When you begin to focus on strengthening your relationship with God, ask yourself a simple question: *Is this bringing me closer to Him?* That's the question I started asking myself about a year after returning to the Church. There were things in my life I needed to look at, not addictions necessarily, but attachments. My phone, food, social media, money, alcohol, and exercise. All of it became fair game.

If I wanted to grow closer to Christ Jesus, I had to take an honest look at what was getting my attention. During Lent 2023, I began letting go of some of those attachments, especially those tied to my phone. I deleted most of my apps, including all social media, and kept only what I truly needed for daily life: email, maps, banking, and a few others. And in 2024, I stopped drinking alcohol altogether. Not because I felt I had a problem with it, but because it didn't align with my health and fitness goals. And it most certainly didn't bring me any closer to God. That examination of attachments has improved my physical and mental well-being, but more than anything, it's helped me make space to become a better disciple.

I've discussed prayer throughout this book, but I want to offer a bit more here, not as an expert, but as someone trying to live it out. Prayer has been one of the most meaningful aspects of my return to the Church, but also one of the hardest to maintain consistency.

Don't get me wrong, I pray every morning. I read the daily scriptures, watch short reflections, and pray the Rosary or other devotions throughout the week, depending on the season. But listening to God—that's the real challenge for me. And when I talk with others, I've learned I'm not alone. Most of us struggle with prayer in one way or another.

I have to remind myself that God isn't asking for perfect words. He wants honest ones. Just speak to Him like you'd talk to anyone you love. If you're tired or in a spiritual dry spell, simply begin with "God, I'm here." Be vulnerable. He already knows what you need, probably better than you do. But telling Him you love Him, and that you're grateful for His mercy and forgiveness, is often all He wants to hear.

Ask for what you need—for yourself, for others. Ask for the strength to forgive, and the grace to understand what He's asking of you. That's prayer. Even just sitting silently in front of the tabernacle is a form of prayer.

Let go of the need to 'feel something' every time you pray. Sometimes, listening to God won't sound like words at all. It may take time. Like any other relationship, it can feel awkward at first, but over time, it becomes more natural. God is steady, even when we aren't.

Over time, I've learned it's not about long or perfect prayers. It's about building small anchors throughout the day. Simple ways to stay connected to God in the middle of real life. That structure has helped me stay grounded, especially when emotions fade or distractions creep in.

For me, the foundation of all prayer is gratitude, expressed with humility. Maybe not theologically, but definitely in practice. I try to begin each morning by thanking God before I do anything else. I thank Him for the day, for His mercy, and for the people in my life. That simple act helps center me. It reminds me that I'm not in control, and that everything I have is a gift. From there, I offer up everything ahead—my work, my thoughts, my struggles, and the good things that might come during the day. It's not just a habit. It's how I stay close to God: by starting with thanks and remembering who I am before Him.

At night, just before I fall asleep, I try to end my day with prayer. It's a final anchor—one last moment to place the day in God's hands. I thank Him again for the joy, the provision, the protection, and even the struggles that pulled me closer to Him. Then I reflect on where I fell short. Sometimes it's the words I didn't say with love. Or the distractions that got in the way. Or the times I wasn't as kind or patient as I should have been. I just ask for His mercy and the grace to do better. Before I fall asleep, I ask Him to bless me through the night and help me live a little more faithfully tomorrow. Ending the day this way brings peace, humility, and perspective.

I'm still figuring out how to read scripture in a way that feels meaningful. And I know I'm not alone. A lot of people struggle here. It's easy to feel like you're doing it wrong. But remember, God meets us where we are. He just asks us to show up honestly.

Approach scripture as a conversation, not a chore. When I first heard this, it helped me a great deal. Daily readings are a good place to start. However, reading through the entire Bible can also provide a broader perspective, especially on the relationship between the Old and New Testaments. One of the first Bibles I picked up after returning was the *Great Adventure Catholic Bible* by Ascension. It uses a color-coded timeline and includes helpful articles, charts, and maps.

Not long after returning to the Church, a friend introduced *Lectio Divina* to Mary Beth and me. It came up again in RCIA, and the more I heard about it, the more it resonated with me. *Lectio*

Divina—"divine reading"—is a simple, meditative way to pray with Scripture. It's not complicated. It offers a peaceful, focused way to spend time with God through His Word.

You start by picking a passage of scripture, such as a passage from the Gospels or a reading from Mass. Read it through once to get a sense of what's happening. Then reread it, much more slowly, paying attention to any words or phrases that stand out. Pause and reflect. What is this saying to me? How does it connect with my life right now? Next, talk honestly with God about whatever comes up—your hopes, questions, worries, or anything stirred by the reading. Finally, take a moment to sit quietly. You don't have to force deep thoughts or feelings; simply let God's word rest in your heart, and let yourself be open to His presence.

I don't use *Lectio Divina* every time I read, but when I do, it helps me slow down and listen. It's not about getting all the answers in one sitting. It's about creating space for God to speak over time. It's not about saying more. It's about listening better.

So what do we do when prayer feels flat? When motivation is low, and nothing seems to connect?

Keep returning.

That's the answer. Just keep returning.

I've come to realize that prayer isn't always an emotional experience. Sometimes it's simply learning something new about scripture. Other times it's silence. Stillness. Maybe just reading the Psalms. God can handle our frustration. He already knows we're distracted. What matters is that we continue to show up.

Alongside prayer, the Mass is where our relationship with God deepens most fully. It's the heart of Catholic life. Through the Liturgy of the Word, and especially through the Eucharist, we encounter Christ in a direct and personal way. But that encounter depends on our full participation, when we show up with intention, listen closely, and receive with faith.

So what does "full participation" look like?

It may vary slightly for each of us. But first, make it a priority to attend Mass each week, whether on Sunday or at the Saturday Vigil. That's non-negotiable. Unless we're too sick to make it, caring for someone who's seriously ill, or truly required to work, we should be at Mass. And if your parish offers daily Mass, try to go at least once during the week. I've found that attending a midweek Mass is a great way to reset when life gets busy or stressful.

We can also prepare in advance. Read the day's scripture readings before Mass. Ask God to show you what He wants you to hear. During Mass, stay engaged. Listen. Join in the responses. Sing the hymns—even if you can't carry a tune.

For years, when I attended Protestant churches, I never sang. Ever. Now I realize I'm not singing for me or anyone around me. I'm singing for God. No matter how I sound.

The longer I'm back in the Church, the more I realize how much I missed having a church family. So, embrace the communal side of the faith. Mass isn't meant to be a solo experience. We pray together, worship together, and grow as a community. Being part of a parish family helps us stay connected to God and to one another.

When we shift our approach from just showing up to being fully engaged, Mass becomes more than an obligation. It becomes a living encounter with Christ.

As you've probably noticed, I've mentioned more than once in this book the importance of simply showing up. A priest in my area, well known throughout the Archdiocese of Atlanta, is famous for saying, "Some days, God just gets my body." I first heard it from my priest, and it stuck with me.

Some days, our hearts are full. Other days, we're tired or distracted. But even then—*especially* then—just showing up is enough. Because when we say yes to God, even when all we can offer is our presence, we're still exactly where we need to be.

STAYING SPIRITUALLY GROUNDED IN A NOISY, DIVIDED WORLD

Once we return to the Church and begin growing in our Catholic faith, we quickly realize that the world around us isn't getting any quieter. If anything, it's noisier than ever. Distractions are constant, especially in the digital space. There's an endless stream of Catholic content online, and while much of it is helpful, some of it isn't. It can be hard to know which voices to trust, which teachings are authentic, and which ones tend to add more confusion than clarity. Even keeping up with Catholic news can feel overwhelming in a Church and a culture that often seems divided.

So, how do we stay grounded? How can we protect our peace, build healthy digital habits, and become more discerning about the Catholic content we take in?

In this hyper-connected world, staying centered in our faith takes intention. One practical place to begin is by setting boundaries around technology, especially screen time. Limiting screen time in the morning, taking simple prayer walks during the day, and resisting the urge to squeeze in prayer between tasks can make a real difference. When prayer becomes just another item on the to-do list, it's easy for other distractions to take over. If we want to grow spiritually, we need to be intentional about making space for God throughout our day.

I shared earlier that I made some changes a few years ago in how I use my phone. That's because I felt like it was getting too much of my attention and pulling me away from God. At the time, I was especially concerned about the impact social media was having on my spiritual life. I started noticing how often I would scroll without thinking, or how quickly I'd reach for my phone whenever I had a quiet moment. It wasn't just a distraction; it was crowding out the stillness I needed for prayer, reflection, and simply being present.

So I started deleting apps. Social media was the first to go. I didn't want to keep filling my mind with endless noise, opinions, and comparisons. I realized that while not all of it was harmful, very little of it was helping me grow. And I didn't want something as small and ordinary as a phone to have that kind of hold on my attention.

Does it still get in the way sometimes? Sure. But by clearing out most of the apps and being more intentional about how often I use them, I've made more room in my life: for God, for peace, for my family, and for the small things He may be trying to say.

Building healthier digital habits can have a tangible impact on our well-being, including our spiritual life. With so much negativity in the world, it's even more important to stay grounded in faith. Setting boundaries around social media and news is a good start, but it's the mindless scrolling that often does the most harm. It pulls us in without purpose and leaves us feeling restless or anxious, often without knowing why. Pay attention to what leaves you feeling depleted, negative, or agitated. Then take a step back. Consider cutting back or cutting it out altogether.

One thing we all need to be more mindful of is comparison, especially when it comes to online content. It's easy to see someone who appears more knowledgeable, more prayerful, or more "Catholic" than we are and start to feel like we're falling short. But like the negativity I mentioned earlier, comparison can slowly chip away at our peace. It can leave us feeling discouraged, inadequate, or spiritually stuck.

The truth is, learning about our faith and growing closer to God looks different for everyone. There's no single path or perfect pace. What matters is staying rooted in your relationship with God, not someone else's. Be a student, yes. Be inspired by others. But don't measure your journey against theirs. God isn't asking you to be a copy of anyone else. He's asking you to be a faithful disciple right where you are.

Many returning Catholics turn to media to learn, catch up, or stay connected to the faith, and that can be beneficial. There are many reliable Catholic voices and trustworthy resources. When used wisely, media can help us grow in understanding and stay rooted in what's happening around the world, not just politically or socially, but through the lens of our faith. Still, if we're not careful, it's easy to get swept up in us-versus-them language: conservative, liberal, traditional, progressive. These are political terms, not Godly ones. And if we start to view the Church through ideological labels, we risk replacing Jesus with opinion.

So what should we watch out for?

Be cautious of content that stirs division or outrage. Good Catholic content should invite us to reflect, not react. It should encourage truth, not fear. I tend to avoid any online voice that spends more time criticizing than uniting, especially if it claims to represent the "real" or "true" Church while attacking others. That's not how the Holy Spirit speaks.

I recently read that discernment isn't just something we do occasionally. It's a habit we have to develop as part of our spiritual life. And it's not just about fact-checking or steering clear of bad content. Discernment is about learning how to recognize the presence of God. It means becoming more aware of what draws us closer to Him, and what pulls us away. If something unsettles you or leaves you feeling uneasy, that might be a sign to pause. Take a moment to pray and reflect before accepting it as truth. The Holy Spirit doesn't speak through fear, confusion, or pride. He speaks through peace, clarity, and love. Learning to recognize that difference is part of what helps us stay grounded in our faith.

I encourage you to ask questions like, "Does this voice sound like Christ?" Will this person or platform bring me closer to God? Will it help me grow in humility, love, and charity—or just deepen my opinions and judgments? Does it leave me at peace, or more reactive?

How do we know where to turn for news, which voices to follow, and what Catholic content is actually worth our time?

First, look for sources that are firmly rooted in the teachings of the Church, such as the Catechism, Scripture, and sacramental life. The focus should always lead back to loving God and loving our neighbor. Trustworthy content doesn't just inform; it builds up. It points us toward truth, not division. You might also lean on sources directly connected to a diocese, the Vatican, or a reputable Catholic publisher or organization. Places where content is more likely to reflect the Church's full teaching and not just one person's opinion.

Not everyone will agree with this, but I recommend avoiding media sources that lean too far in either direction. The most helpful content is measured and centered. It minimizes bias and offers thoughtful, faithful commentary on what's happening in the Church and the world. As a general rule, if a source seems more focused on stirring controversy than offering insight, it's probably not helping you grow closer to God. If you're ever unsure, talk with your priest, check with your diocese, or consult the United States Conference of Catholic Bishops (USCCB) for guidance.

There's more online Catholic content available now than ever before, and that can be helpful. It makes learning easier and helps us stay connected. But we need to be careful. We don't return to our Catholic faith to join a team. This isn't about picking sides or falling into camps. We're here to follow Christ. We belong to one, universal Church, founded by Christ, rooted in truth, and held together in faith and community. Let that be your compass as you explore, learn, and grow in the faith.

WELCOMING OTHERS BACK TO THE CHURCH

As we continue to grow in our faith, it's natural to want to help others find their way too. That's how the idea for this book began. When I went looking for a practical guide for returning Catholics, I couldn't find one that fit my experience. So I started writing the kind of resource I wish I'd had—something honest, relatable, and grounded in real life.

You don't need a theology degree or a perfect faith life to help someone return to the Church. You just need to be honest about where you are, how you got here, and what might help someone else navigate their own return. Your story, lived and shared with humility, is your greatest invitation.

When someone sees that you've come back to the Catholic faith and are living it out with sincerity, it speaks louder than anything scripted. People are drawn to authenticity. You don't need to have all the right words or perfect answers. By living your faith with quiet consistency, you may inspire someone else to take their first step. They might be watching to see if this change in your life is real, or wondering if there's hope for them to come back too. Let your experience be the nudge they've been waiting for. And when the time comes, don't be afraid to share it, not to convince or impress, but simply to say: I've been there too. And I found my way home.

People connect more with real experiences than with rehearsed lines. The power of testimony can't be overstated. You still don't need to have it all figured out. Just be sincere, and others will listen. Your story may be exactly what they needed to hear.

Over time, I've found it helpful to have more than one version of my story. A brief version, perhaps 30 seconds, works well in casual conversations. A longer version might be more appropriate when someone is genuinely curious and wants to hear the whole story: why I left the Church, what drew me back, and what it's been like since my return. I've also learned that I don't need to share everything all at once. A few key details can often go further than a long explanation. If you share just enough to spark curiosity or offer hope, that's often enough to open a door.

It also helps to let others know that returning to the Church may be a longer process. For many of us, it unfolds slowly. It's a gradual reawakening of faith over time. That's how I experienced it. That kind of honesty makes your story more relatable. It helps others feel less alone in whatever they might be wrestling with. It also helps normalize the process.

And there's no need to come across as overly religious or polished. Just be yourself. People are far more likely to be drawn to a faith that feels sincere and genuine than one that comes off as forced or inauthentic.

It's also interesting how people often notice that you are at peace before anything else. A few months after I returned to the Church, someone came up to me after Mass and asked, "When did you first know you'd come back? You seem at peace, and everything about you shows you're happy." He was worried about his adult children, who were around my age, and just needed to know it's possible for someone to return to the Catholic faith later in life. This was long before I started sharing my story with others, but his question gave me the freedom to open up about what I'd been through and how God had led me home. Looking back, I think that moment was the beginning of something more profound—God was planting the seeds of what would later become my calling to help other fallen-away Catholics, including through the work of this book.

I've also had to learn when to speak and when to listen. There will be times when it's better to invite someone else to tell their own story. Ask about their background, how they see God, or what faith has meant to them. Share your own story when it feels natural and safe. And it's always okay to say, "I'm still figuring it out too." That kind of honesty builds trust.

Sometimes, the most powerful thing you can do is simply listen. Listening with compassion and understanding is one of the most meaningful forms of witness. In a world where so many feel unheard, giving someone the space to share their story shows they matter. You're not trying to fix them. You're just being present. And that kind of presence can open the door to trust, healing, and maybe even faith.

When you do feel ready to share your story, it's often best to start small. A simple invitation to Mass can go a long way. So can sharing what's helped you: "I've been going to Adoration lately. Let me know if you'd ever want to check it out." Take on a no-pressure mindset. People return to the Church for various reasons, and this often happens gradually, sometimes over years. Your job isn't to convince or rush them. It's to extend a hand.

And if they say no, don't be discouraged. A simple invitation can stay with someone longer than you think. Even if they don't act on it right away—or at all—just knowing they were welcomed might matter more than you realize. Trust that God is still working, even in silence, even in hesitation.

Telling your story can also help more than just former Catholics who are considering returning to the faith. It can resonate with anyone, regardless of background or belief, who is struggling with faith or searching for meaning. When someone hears how you found your way back to God, it reminds them that it's never too late. A sincere story of grace and renewal can make faith feel reachable again for someone unsure where to start.

It could be that you're the person someone else has been silently waiting for. Your return to the Catholic faith might give them the courage to ask questions or take a step they've been putting off for years. Something you say, or simply the way you live, might help open that door. That's the beauty of returning. It's not just about us. It's about offering hope that the door is still open for everyone.

7

Keeping the Faith
A Lifelong Pilgrimage

IN THE LAST CHAPTER, we explored how to live out our Catholic faith in everyday life—through prayer, community, service, and helping others who are searching. In this chapter, we'll explore what it takes to make that faith last, not just in times of spiritual energy or clarity, but also through seasons of doubt, dryness, or uncertainty.

Over time, faith stops feeling new or emotional. What once felt exciting can start to feel ordinary, even routine. That's when discouragement can creep in, or when you may wonder if your devotion is fading. Doubts may return. Periods of spiritual distance may come. Life may still get messy. But faith was never meant to rest on constant emotion. It's about staying the course with God, trusting His presence, even when the path feels unclear.

A steady faith takes intention, trust, and the discipline to remain present, even when it's hard.

IF DOUBT OR STRUGGLE RETURN

Not a day goes by that I don't thank God for calling me back to the Catholic Church. But I wish I could say that once you return, everything settles into place and your spiritual life clicks into gear. That hasn't been my experience, and I don't think it's the norm. Life keeps happening. And often, the deeper work of faith begins after you return.

Even after returning to the Church, you may still wrestle with new questions or lingering uncertainties. That doesn't mean you've taken a wrong turn. It just means you're paying attention. You're growing. And while you might assume that by now you should feel steady and sure, it's normal to feel unsettled in some areas of your faith.

The journey isn't always linear. Sometimes what feels like slipping is really God drawing you further along the path. Doubt doesn't always mean you're disagreeing with the Church's teachings. Sometimes it simply means God hasn't revealed something to you yet. Continue to pray for the gift of insight and understanding. I once read that belief and doubt can coexist in the same heart. I've found that to be true.

As the father in Mark 9:24 says, *"I believe; help my unbelief."*

Because God desires an intimate relationship with us more than anything, he will always meet us right where we are—even in the middle of doubt, frustration, or confusion. He's not waiting for us to have perfect answers or a complete understanding. He is with us in the struggle.

Don't hide your questions. Don't be afraid to bring your doubts to God. Bring it to him, fully and honestly, without pretending. That's where grace often begins. Not in having it all figured out, but in the quiet, ongoing conversation we have with our Father. That personal dialogue is where faith deepens, even when the road feels unclear.

Since my return, I've expected to feel more settled than I did. I've had doubts. I've struggled with specific Church teachings, and I've struggled in prayer. But I always bring those struggles to God. I ask him to show me what I'm not yet seeing. I ask for the grace to stay focused and patient, especially in prayer, when it feels difficult or dry. On the days when prayer doesn't come easily, I sometimes worry I'm not being as faithful as I should be. But even in those moments, I know God is there too. I've had to remind myself that if I keep turning toward Him, he'll lead me forward.

If you're back in the Church but still feel unsure about some things—or even wonder at times where you stand with God—you're not alone. Many people experience this. Coming back doesn't mean every question disappears, or that your relationship with God will always feel on solid ground. These moments of uncertainty aren't a sign that you're failing. They're often part of learning how to stay.

Faith that lasts is not built overnight. It grows over time. It takes root in the ups and downs, through prayer, perseverance, and the steady decision to keep turning back to God. Doubt isn't the opposite of faith. It becomes part of how faith matures, as you learn to trust God even when you don't have all the answers.

While working on this chapter, I came across something that surprised me. Mother Teresa spent many decades of her life feeling far from God. Even as she cared for the poor and lived a life of prayer, she often felt like God was absent. She carried that spiritual desolation quietly for years. What struck me most was that she never gave up. She kept praying. She kept serving. And through it all, she stayed faithful, even when she didn't feel close to God.

Learning that gave me hope—not just for myself, but for all of us. If someone like her could feel distant from God and still stay committed, then maybe those times of struggle don't mean we're doing something wrong. Perhaps they're just part of the journey. Her story reminded me that faith isn't always about feeling close to God. It's about staying with him, even when he feels far away.

Having faith in God doesn't mean being perfect or having all the answers. There's a common thread here. Stay on your path, keep showing up, and continue seeking the truth through God's word. If you can do that, you're further along than you think.

STAYING ROOTED IN THE SACRAMENTS

Many of us return to the Church through the sacraments. They're often the gateway back—tangible encounters with God that guide us home. But the sacraments don't just mark our return. They become the way we stay Catholic.

This section focuses on how the sacraments, particularly the Eucharist and Reconciliation, sustain us throughout the long journey of our lives. They aren't just milestones or rituals. They're lifelines, offering nourishment, renewal, and stability when life feels messy or faith feels dry. The sacraments aren't just symbols or sacred moments. They're genuine encounters with Christ. When we take part in them, we're not simply remembering Jesus. We're meeting Him. He's truly present, offering us grace that transforms us from the inside out. Whether you're strong in your spiritual life or struggling to stay consistent, making space for the sacraments is one of the most grounding practices we have as Catholics.

Over the past several years, I've come to see the sacraments differently. Early on, I saw them mainly as the way back—a path of return and the way to eternal salvation. And they are. But now I understand something more. The sacraments hold us steady. They don't just welcome us home. They keep us rooted in Christ and connected to His Church.

There will be times when our spiritual life feels empty and we sense some distance from God. That experience is more common than we often admit, especially in today's busy world. In those moments, it's important to remember that the sacraments are at work in our lives, no matter how we feel. They continue shaping us, even when we feel nothing at all. They aren't meant to elevate our mood; they are how we receive healing and grace. I've gone through periods when prayer felt flat, yet I still received the Eucharist. I've hesitated at times to go to confession, but I went. And even in the struggle, the sacraments still gave me what I needed most—grace and restoration.

At the heart of why I'm Catholic is the Eucharist. Together with Reconciliation, it anchors my spiritual life and shapes the rhythm of my faith week after week. It's not uncommon for me to feel emotional during this part of the Mass. Sometimes it's overwhelming to consider just how great a gift it is. The Eucharist grounds us, even when we show up distracted or disconnected.

When I first returned after being away for so many years, the Eucharist took on a deep meaning for me. What I want to emphasize here is what it continues to do for us throughout our lives. It helps us become more like Christ. You don't have to be perfect or feel especially holy to receive the Eucharist. What matters most is coming with an open heart and a willingness to believe that Christ is truly present.

The Eucharist nourishes us, even when we don't realize it. On the days we feel spiritually connected and on the days we don't, grace is still being given. I think of it like the food we eat. We don't always know how it's nourishing us—we just know that it does. That's how I've come to see the Eucharist. It gives us life, sustains us, and renews our commitment to Christ and our Catholic faith. We were never meant to be present with our Lord and receive His Body and Blood only occasionally. The Church invites us to return often because this is how we stay close to Christ. If you're fortunate to have daily Mass nearby, consider going as often as possible.

Revisiting the sacrament of Reconciliation, it's worth saying again: this sacrament doesn't just heal and restore; it reshapes us over time. That's why it matters to go more than once a year, if possible. Guilt, anxiety, and a sense of spiritual distance can begin to build over time. Reconciliation is not only about confessing what we've done, but it's about remembering who we are as children of God. The feelings that follow confession—relief, clarity, and being realigned with God—often give us the strength to persevere when our spiritual life feels challenging. Even on those tough days, the sacraments continue to work. When you're feeling stuck, Reconciliation clears the path. Grace keeps flowing.

Staying rooted in the sacraments doesn't require getting everything right. It requires honesty and a habit of returning. Life gets busy. Maybe even a little chaotic at times. There may be times you miss Mass. Other times, you put off confession. And sometimes you even feel distant from God. *That's when it matters most to reconnect.* Even after long gaps, we're always invited to return.

Sometimes the drift isn't years long. It's just a few busy months when prayer slides or Mass gets missed. Those lapses matter too, but they don't have to derail us. The invitation is the same—return, even in small steps. Go back to Mass this Sunday. Pick up prayer again tomorrow. Grace builds quickly when we take that first step back.

Yes, over time, when we've been away from the sacraments, especially Reconciliation, guilt can creep in. Sometimes it feels like an unseen burden. Other times, it turns into shame. But that shame never comes from God. It rises from within us. It's not punishment. It's a signal. A reminder that God is still waiting for us.

Returning to the sacraments, even when you don't feel ready, is itself an act of trust. It's a way of saying, *"I believe God's grace is bigger than any doubt or failure I might have."* When we participate in the sacraments, we always grow closer to God. And as we draw closer to Him, our trust deepens. We begin to rely on His grace more than on our own strength.

What keeps us rooted in the sacraments isn't how often we go, but the desire that brings us back. There will be times when routines slip or when faith feels dim. What matters most is not how far we've drifted. It's that we turn toward God again and again. The sacraments are always ready to meet us. And so is God.

I see the core, daily sacraments not as check-ins or obligations, but as how I reset and reorient my heart to God. It has been a great relief to realize they are always working, even on the days when I don't feel strong or fully present.

I invite you to reflect on the following. If you've already returned to the Church, think about what the sacraments have meant in your life since then. Have there been times when you almost didn't go to Mass or confession, but went anyway? What did that moment reveal to you? Often, it is in the small decisions we make, especially when we don't feel ready or motivated, that the sacraments do their deepest work. Each time we return, they help steady us. Each time God works through the sacraments, we are drawn closer to Him. And that is what He wants most of all.

STAYING THE COURSE WHEN FAITH FEELS DRY

There may come a time in your faith life when things feel a little off. Many people experience it as dryness or a sense of disconnection. Others describe it as a time when God seems quiet. They don't feel heard, and they can't seem to hear Him either. Sometimes it appears as a kind of tension or restlessness that's hard to explain. When this happens, it's easy to wonder if you're doing something wrong.

But I've read about this experience, talked with others, and lived it myself, and I can tell you it's completely normal. It happens to devoted, prayerful people—even the saints.

So if you've ever found yourself in this place, know this without a doubt: *you're not doing anything wrong*. It doesn't mean you're not trying hard enough. And it certainly doesn't mean you've lost your faith. This isn't a sign that your faith is failing. If anything, it's a sign that you're walking the long road of discipleship that lasts a lifetime.

There can be many triggers of these periods of spiritual struggle. I'm not talking about isolated moments here and there, but those longer stretches of dryness that show up from time to time. Often, they're tied to life disruptions, such as illness, stress at work or home, disappointment, or even plain fatigue. Sometimes the cause is more external: changes in your parish, a new priest with a very different style, or even instability in the Church more broadly. Conflicting messaging, news stories, or a transition in leadership, such as the appointment of a new bishop or pope, can all impact how we feel as practicing Catholics.

For some, the struggle isn't just internal. It's disillusionment or even hurt caused by experiences in their parish or the wider Church. That kind of pain can make showing up even harder. Yet even in those moments, Christ's presence in the sacraments remains the same. He is unchanging and faithful, even when people or institutions fall short.

Even positive changes can leave us feeling unsettled simply because they're unfamiliar. Whatever the reason, it helps to notice what triggers this dryness for you. Awareness can't prevent every difficult stretch, but it can help you be more proactive in staying connected, especially through the sacraments and prayer. For instance, if you notice that stress at work tends to pull you away from prayer, you might carve out a few minutes at lunch for silent reflection or a short scripture reading. Small acts of awareness can keep you from drifting too far for too long.

It's comforting to know that many saints and Church leaders have gone through these same struggles. Mother Teresa experienced decades of what she called 'spiritual darkness,' all while continuing to serve the poor. In her case, it wasn't an absence of faith but a profound sense of distance from God. Her faith endured—not because it always felt strong, but because she kept returning.

Pope Benedict XVI frequently spoke and wrote about the spiritual challenges that accompany faith, including periods of uncertainty and inner struggle faced by all believers. He often used images like 'storms' and 'darkness,' not only to describe his experience leading the Church through turbulent times, but also to describe the personal journey of faith. In his reflections, he reminded us that faith isn't about constant clarity or peace. It's about staying rooted in Christ, especially when things feel uncertain. He emphasized that real growth begins when we let go of the need to understand everything and start learning to trust.

His life and teachings point us to something simple yet lasting: even when faith feels weak, it is still faith. Sometimes it's as small as praying when you don't feel like it, walking into Mass when it feels ordinary, or simply saying, "Help me, Lord" in the middle of a difficult day. Those little choices, repeated, are what keep faith alive.

Even Father Mike Schmitz, one of the most well-known Catholic voices today, has spoken about the reality of spiritual dryness. From what I've heard and read, he often emphasizes that these tough stretches aren't just common; they may even be necessary. They can purify the heart, strip away distractions, and draw us back to what matters most.

He also frequently points to the Catechism, which reminds us that "prayer is a battle" *(Catechism of the Catholic Church, 2nd ed.,*

2725). That line has stayed with me. There's no promise that prayer will always feel peaceful or come easily—only the truth. Prayer takes effort. It asks for a decision to keep showing up, even when nothing seems to happen. And sometimes that's exactly where the real work of faith begins.

Tough stretches in our prayer life matter more than we think. If we approach them with humility, they can become growth opportunities. One of the first things we learn is that we're not in complete control of our spiritual well-being. That can be a hard realization, but it also teaches trust. We begin to see that God is always in control, and our job is to continually turn to Him, regardless of our feelings. Dryness can reveal how much we've come to rely on feelings or comfortable circumstances to feel close to God. When those things fall away, the real question becomes: will I show up anyway? And if we do, if we keep showing up in faith even when it's hard, we often discover that God has been working in us all along, even if we couldn't feel it.

Finding an anchor in Christ is essential, especially in times of dryness. In those seasons, we have to return to what keeps us steady—prayer and the sacraments. When we stay close to Him there, trust tends to hold firm. But when prayer fades or the sacraments are neglected, that trust can slowly weaken. That's why the darker seasons are the very moments when prayer and the sacraments matter most.

Staying attuned to the Church's liturgical calendar can also help us. Just as nature moves through seasons, the Church walks us through a cycle of feasts, fasts, and holy days. Following the liturgical calendar gives us a steady point of reference throughout the year. It keeps our faith life connected to Christ, even when things seem to be distracting us.

Each season invites us into something different: penance, preparation, celebration, hope. Even when we feel stuck, the Church continues to move forward. It offers direction when we're unsure how to pray or how to show up. Lent may stretch us when we're ready for renewal. Ordinary Time gives us some space to breathe and reflect. Advent can bring stillness when life feels chaotic. It's not just about marking time. It's about staying connected to the larger story of salvation, even when our own story feels uncertain.

And when personal prayer feels dry, the Church continues to pray with us and for us through daily Mass, offering structure, meaning, and a sense of movement when we need it most.

Even in the short time I've been back in the Church, I've had stretches of uncertainty and doubt. I've found that the sacraments help keep my faith clear and steady. But I have also found strength by attending Bible study at my parish and being part of a Catholic men's group. Studying scripture and discussing spiritual questions with others is always helpful. And there's something especially meaningful about the people God has placed around me, those I see each week at church, at Bible study, and in the men's group. In difficult times, they've often been the ones who inspire me to keep going, simply by the way they show up, remain faithful, and continue pursuing Christ.

I'll end this section with this reassurance: if you find yourself in a stretch of dryness or struggle in your faith, it doesn't mean you're failing. It may mean you're growing. As the saying goes, "In a storm, roots matter more than branches." And that's what we're growing as we continue walking with Christ.

CENTERED FOR THE JOURNEY

As we close this chapter, I want to be honest: returning to the Church doesn't make every hardship disappear. Life will still bring moments of grief, conflict, regret, and uncertainty. Yet it also brings something hopeful, a center you can always return to, built on Christ, the sacraments, and His Church. That changes everything. Before my return, those same struggles felt confusing, even overwhelming. Now I face them with a different heart. Coming back hasn't just given me more tools; it's changed who I turn to first. This isn't about avoiding the hard places in life. It's about walking through them with a new center. It means that when challenges come, you aren't scrambling to find footing. You already know where to stand, and *Who* to lean on.

When we speak of being "centered" in your return to the Catholic faith, we mean it in the most profound sense. It's found in all the sacraments, the teachings of the Church, the support of our parish, and the presence of Christ in all of it. There's a significant shift. You are no longer navigating hardships alone but are held by something greater. And we should find much hope in that.

Being Christ-centered changes how we live each day. It shapes the way we pray, handle challenges at work or home, and respond when life takes an unexpected turn. It gives us the grace to forgive when it's hard, the humility to ask for help, and the assurance that God has a plan even when we don't see it. Challenges will still come, but now we face them grounded in Christ and the life of the Church. Having this firm foundation doesn't mean life will feel comfortable; it means there's spiritual stability even in discomfort.

Returning opens doors to healing old wounds and gaining clarity for the road ahead. But most long-term change happens slowly. In my own life, I've held onto a specific image that keeps me steady when challenges arise. In my first year back, it felt as if a veil had been lifted. I could see with new clarity the life God intended for me. When challenges arise, I picture Christ standing beside me, His hand on my shoulder. That's the image I carry. Remembering that image has calmed my heart in tense moments, given me courage in difficult conversations, and reminded me that His strength is greater than my weakness.

Surrendering your life to the Lord is daily work—it won't happen all at once. When we trust God and remain faithful to the process, our relationship with Him deepens. That trust grows as we continue to show up in prayer and receive the sacraments. When we drift from those daily anchors, a quiet distance forms, not because God has moved away but because we have stepped back. And in those moments, trust can feel out of reach.

This is how we keep the faith over a lifetime. We move from drifting through life with uncertainty or anxiety to living with a steady, enduring confidence in God. An inner stability develops over time, founded in Christ and the Church. That stability sustains us through the dry or uncertain seasons we talked about in the previous section, and it carries us through our whole lives as practicing Catholic Christians. When the storms come—and they will—you know you have an anchor. And over time, that anchor becomes more than security in a storm; it becomes the constant presence that shapes how you live every day.

I've seen firsthand how being centered in Christ changes my responses, even when life doesn't get easier. One example is how I now handle difficult people: those who bully, speak harshly about others, or seem to carry a constant cloud of negativity. When I encounter this, I pray, *"God, grant me the grace to see this world, and others, through Your love-filled eyes."* That brief prayer resets my perspective. It reminds me that every person, regardless of their actions, is someone God loves. My faith helps me better respond with patience, gentleness, or sometimes not respond at all. In the past, I would have been quick to judge or confront. Centering myself in Christ doesn't make those moments pleasant, but it changes me. And often, that change shifts the tone of the moment too.

Earlier, I shared how others inspired me during my struggles with faith. They've become more than fellow parishioners—they're friends and family in the truest sense. Beyond the inevitable dry seasons, a strong faith community helps keep us centered when life gets messy. Sometimes it's through a simple prayer or word of encouragement. Other times, it's the honesty of accountability or a gentle push back toward the sacraments. This kind of shared faith and care is how Jesus designed His Church from the very beginning. One of the surest ways to stay close to Him is to walk with other believers in a committed, Christ-centered community of faith. Whether it's through serving together, studying Scripture, or simply sharing life's ups and downs, these relationships keep us rooted when we might otherwise drift.

The real story of our return to the Catholic faith isn't just about coming back. It's about staying and remaining faithful to Christ and His Church throughout a lifetime. You're not just another fallen-away Catholic who came home. You are someone who stays, who trusts, who commits, and who shares your story so others might find their way back too.

Returning to the Church doesn't remove the hard edges of life, but it gives us a steady ground to stand on. Rooted in Christ, strengthened by the sacraments, and encouraged by those who walk with us, we find the clarity and courage to keep moving forward.

8

When the People You Love Are Far From Faith

When I speak with others in the Church or those who have returned to their Catholic faith, I find that many share the same quiet concern. Their adult children, grandchildren, or other loved ones have drifted away from faith. This chapter is an honest conversation about that worry, including the regret some of us feel for not having led spiritually as well as we could have. I've said this myself; I should have been a better spiritual leader in my family and community, especially with my children. If you've felt the same, I want to offer encouragement, a reminder that you're not alone, and a few practical ways to live out your faith without feeling pressured. God is still at work, and we have to trust His timing.

THE PART THAT STILL HURTS

You've returned to the Church. You're grateful. But a part of you still feels unsettled. Many of us still carry the hurt of watching our children or grandchildren drift from faith, even though they were raised as Christians. And then comes the tricky, unspoken question: *What did I do wrong? Am I at fault?*

For some of us, like me, there are things we could have done better. For others, the answer may be *nothing*. Their loved ones simply made different choices as they entered adulthood. People choose their own paths, no matter how they were raised. Some of us carry regret. Others may not know exactly what to feel.

All of that is normal. And it's more common than we might think. Many of us carry the weight of wishing we had done more. Coming back to the Church can make the spiritual separation from our loved ones feel even harder, especially when we see a new generation growing up with little or no connection to God or the sacraments. Just know that this is a deeply human experience. Both joy and sadness can coexist. It's not a failure of faith, but a reality many returning Catholics carry in their hearts.

The answer to these questions isn't always clear. Some of us know we did the best we could with the time, energy, and understanding we had. Others carry a burden that doesn't go away so easily. We regret not making faith a true priority in those busy years of raising kids and building careers. That's one of my biggest regrets. I rarely emphasized spiritual habits at home. I was inconsistent in my church life. And I seldom spoke about my faith or Catholic roots, even though I often felt close to God and prayed on my own. This isn't to shame anyone. It's simply to say: it's okay to admit where we fell short.

Yes, looking back can be difficult. But at a certain point on our spiritual journey, it becomes necessary. That pain feels stronger now that we've rediscovered the faith we had lost. And we want our families to experience it too, especially our children and grandchildren.

When we step back and reflect on what those we love are missing—faith, the sacraments, a relationship with God—we can't help but feel that distance more deeply. The gap between generations can also feel overwhelming, especially when we see children not being baptized, weddings happening outside the Church, or loved ones growing up without ever having the chance to know Christ Jesus.

It helps to remember that God sees what we cannot. Some of our loved ones may carry wounds, addiction, trauma, or mental illness that we cannot fix. The Church teaches that God's mercy is not limited by these struggles. His grace reaches into places beyond our control, bringing strength and healing in ways we may not see. This truth can bring comfort, reminding us that their story is still held in His hands. Even when our loved ones seem far from faith or unable to come to the Church, God is never far from them.

When I considered adding this chapter, someone mentioned to me the story of Saint Monica and her years of prayer for her son, Augustine. Monica, who lived during the fourth century, spent much of her life praying for the conversion of her family, but especially her son. Augustine was intelligent, but also rebellious, and for many years, he pursued "worldly pleasures" and adopted practices and beliefs that contradicted Christianity.

Monica never gave up. She followed him to different cities, asking Church leaders for guidance along the way. One of them, Bishop Ambrose of Milan, offered advice that stayed with her: "*Speak less to Augustine about God, and more to God about Augustine.*" Monica had already been praying, but that advice deepened her trust in God even more.

Eventually, Augustine came to faith while in Milan, in part through the preaching of Ambrose. In 386, he embraced Christianity and was baptized the following year. Monica, who is now considered the patron saint of mothers, married women, and conversions, died soon after, at peace knowing her son had turned to Christ.

The story of Monica and Augustine is, at its heart, a story of hope. Monica stayed faithful year after year, even when her prayers seemed to go unanswered. She didn't give ultimatums or try to shame Augustine into changing. She simply loved him, stayed present, and prayed without giving up. Her approach may not be one we can all follow, because God works differently in every life. For some of us, our prayers may be answered in ways we don't expect, or not in our lifetime at all. But her example reminds us of something important—prayer matters. Hope matters. Love matters. Even when we can't see progress, God is still at work in ways we may not fully understand.

If this is something you're carrying, I want to reassure you that you aren't alone. You're not the only one praying in silence and holding on to hope that God will draw your loved ones closer to Him. In pews all around you are others with the same quiet ache, lifting up similar prayers and waiting for God to answer. The burden is real, but so is the grace to carry it. That grace meets us in the small moments: when we light a candle, whisper their name in prayer, or when they come to mind during Mass. God sees all of it, and He knows the love behind every prayer.

It's good to turn our focus from what's missing to what's still possible by trusting in Christ Jesus. We can't rewrite the past, but we can be present now: with compassion, patience, and an open heart. God sees you. He knows your hurt. And He will honor your prayers.

Remember, He is not finished with their story.

LIVING FAITH IN PLAIN SIGHT

You've probably had someone recommend a book or movie to you over and over. People mean well and are excited about it, but somehow, the more they mention it, the less interested you become. You begin to feel like it's no longer your choice. It's not that you're being difficult. It's just how we're wired. Psychologists call it *reactance*—that inner resistance we feel when our freedom to choose feels even slightly threatened.

I've experienced that too. The more someone insists I "have to" experience something, the less likely I am to do it. It's not pride or stubbornness; it's human nature. And the same thing can happen in matters of faith. Even when we mean well, repeated pressure can cause others to pull back. And even with the best of intentions, it doesn't always come across that way.

The same thing happens when we try to nudge someone we love toward church or back to faith. No matter how gently we try, it can still feel like pressure. And the more we bring it up, the more likely they are to tune it out. People can't be pushed into faith. It has to be a choice. It's grace, not persuasion, that brings someone home. We want to help them, but we have to remind ourselves that this is God's work, not ours.

This section explores how we navigate that tension. It's about the longing for our loved ones to return to their faith and come back to Mass, and the need to give them space. We want them to experience the beauty of the Church, but we also know that pressuring them rarely helps. Faith grows through freedom, not force. Our role is to continue loving, praying, and trusting that God is at work, even when we can't see it.

I returned to my Catholic faith with no pressure to do so. Sometimes I think it might have happened sooner if I'd had stronger connections in the Catholic community. But looking back now, I know I could only return on God's time, not my own. I had to wait for God to move me, not because someone was constantly pushing me. My return came from a pull I couldn't explain. It was a mix of God's grace, old memories, the sense that something was missing, and finally, that first step forward. The same will be true for others. The grace to find their way home has to unfold gradually and personally, shaped by their story rather than ours.

What I've come to understand is that even when your loved ones aren't interested in church or prayer, they still notice how you live. This is the power of living faith in plain sight. People notice that you attend Mass every week. They notice when you pray before meals, even if no one joins you. They hear the way you speak about others, the tone you use when you're frustrated, and the way you offer forgiveness when it's hard. These moments may feel small, but they often speak more clearly than anything we could say. As the saying goes, *"We may be the only Bible some people ever read."* And how we live out our faith might be what God uses to reach others when the time is right.

There is something powerful about faith in life's ordinary moments. These are the opportunities for simple witness. None of this requires perfection. What matters is being present, staying aware of how we come across to others, and remembering one thing: it's not enough to know Jesus or admire His example. We're called to live it.

Being noticed won't be about others acknowledging or commenting on what they see. And that's completely fine. Just know that others are watching, quietly storing what they see for a time later on when their hearts are ready. Each person's journey to God is deeply personal. Some paths are straight. Others take years of winding. We have to let go of the urge to control timing or outcomes, even when we feel urgency. Faith is not a formula. It unfolds slowly, uniquely, and always in God's time.

We can stay faithful to our journey and trust that God sees all of it. I've been blessed to be around people whose unassuming holiness inspires me. Parishioners who show up early to pray. Priests who live their vocation with steady strength. Even strangers whose kindness reveals something deeper. They're not trying to impress anyone, but their faith shows up in the way they carry themselves. I often pray for the humility to grow in that same direction. Not to be admired, but to become the kind of person God can work through. Sometimes all it takes is one visible life of faith to plant a seed, one that may grow later, maybe much later.

I encourage you to keep living out your faith, even when it feels unseen. What you model in everyday life, such as your patience, prayers, and choices, can shape hearts in ways you may never fully realize. God uses everything you offer. Often, the life you live is the most powerful message you will ever deliver.

GENTLE WAYS TO KEEP THE DOOR OPEN

Up to this point, we've seen that faith shows itself most clearly in the way we live. That steady presence matters. But there are also times when we feel the pull to do something more: small gestures that say "I care about you" without pushing too hard. These aren't tactics to convince someone or change their mind. They're simply ways to keep the door open, to remind our loved ones that we see them, we care for them, and we trust God to guide the rest.

Keeping the door open, to me, is about hope. Not strategies to win someone over. Not pressure until someone finally gives in. This is about love—offering it freely, with no expectations and sometimes without even acknowledgement. Hope without pressure. It means being willing to extend an honest and humble invitation without expecting anything in return. When we long to see our loved ones find or return to faith, being gentle has to remain the most important thing. That's what preserves the relationship and protects trust. And always remember that faith only grows in God's time.

One of the most impactful things we can do is share what our return to the Church has meant to us—especially our personal relationship with Christ. In casual conversations, I sometimes describe it as a kind of "superpower" in my life. Knowing that God is with me is freeing and empowering. Taking small opportunities to share that reality goes a long way without overreaching or sounding preachy. When we've been away from faith for a long time, there's a deep peace in finally realizing what we've been missing. Sharing that feeling, especially through a personal story, can be truly impactful.

If the moment is right, it can also be meaningful to say you're praying for someone. Of course, this won't fit every person or every situation. But sometimes it does. Letting your loved ones know you believe in the power of prayer is about offering reassurance, not guilt. Even a simple "I said a prayer for you today" can be enough to remind someone they are remembered and loved.

Another small way of witnessing is by keeping visible reminders of faith in your home. These items create an environment of belief without words. A crucifix on the wall, a Bible on the nightstand, or a rosary in plain sight might seem ordinary, but they quietly point to what matters most. They don't demand attention or force a conversation. Instead, they signal that your belief in God is sincere and lived. Who knows, maybe a grandchild will notice the crucifix on the wall even if you've never pointed it out. That simple moment could open a natural opportunity to talk about faith. Over time, these reminders can encourage healthy curiosity in your family and open the door to questions or conversations when everyone is ready.

One small step I've taken is inviting my family to join Mary Beth and me at Mass on special occasions, such as Christmas, Easter, or even the Feast of Our Lady of Guadalupe. It's never about pressure. It's just an open invitation, a way of letting them know they are always welcome. Sometimes they say yes, sometimes they don't. Either way, the invitation itself keeps the door open. That's the heart of it—gentle gestures that create space for God to work without us stepping in to manage the outcome.

When invitations are turned down, it's important to accept the answer gracefully. No disappointment. No guilt trips. Sometimes your reaction speaks even louder than the invitation itself. A calm and patient response shows that your love isn't conditional, that you're not keeping score, and that their relationship matters more to you than their attendance at Mass. It also shows that your love doesn't depend on what they choose in that moment.

We invite our loved ones to Mass, but even when they don't come, there are moments within the liturgy itself when we can lift them up in prayer. Naming them silently during the petitions or remembering them as the priest raises the Eucharist is a powerful way to place them before God. The Mass is the highest form of prayer the Church offers, and placing our family members there—at the altar, before Christ himself—is one of the most meaningful ways we can intercede for them. Another step is to have a Mass offered for their intentions. You don't always need to tell them, though sometimes letting them know can be a gift in itself. Either way, offering a Mass places their lives in God's hands in a profound way, reminding us that their story rests with Him.

We often carry this quietly, but we don't have to. One of the gifts of being Catholic is that we pray together. Sharing your intentions for your children or grandchildren with a prayer group, a men's or women's ministry, or even trusted friends is a way of leaning on the strength of the Church community. It reminds us that this burden isn't ours alone. And as they lift up your loved ones, you may also find comfort in praying for their families too. There is strength in knowing that, together, we are asking God to move in the lives of those we love.

In all of this, it can be difficult not to see the change we hope for in those we love. But our part is clear: we witness, we invite, and we shine a light on the good God has already worked in our lives. The rest belongs to Him. That lack of control can feel discouraging, but it is also freeing because we don't have to carry the weight ourselves. Trust His timing. And remember your own story. It took time, and so will theirs.

We're also not the first to struggle with wanting this for our loved ones. The Church has always looked to the saints for encouragement, and their example helps us stay faithful when the wait feels long. Think back to Saint Monica, whose decades of patient prayer for her son Augustine remind us that perseverance and trust can bear fruit in God's time.

Our faithfulness to the Lord extends farther than we will ever see in this life, not only for our own spiritual growth, but also as a reminder to our families and others who have drifted away. Love others. Pray faithfully. Live your faith out loud. God will use even the smallest gestures in ways you may never see.

When those we love are far from faith, know that your prayers and presence are part of God's ongoing work in their lives. Even if you cannot see it now, He is weaving every act of love into His greater plan. One day, you may be surprised to see the fruit God brings from the seeds you've planted.

9

Welcome Home
The Joy of Embracing God's Love

WHAT A JOURNEY THIS has been. In these pages, we've walked through the ache of something missing, the pull to return, the rediscovery of the sacraments, and the call to live faith for the long road ahead. Every step matters, even the ones that feel uncertain or heavy. Nothing is wasted, because God has been present through it all. If you've made it this far, you know what it feels like to wrestle with questions, to carry the weight of being away, and to long for more. And you also know something even greater: that God's love has never left you, and His presence has never stopped walking beside you, no matter where you are on the road.

REFLECTING ON THE JOURNEY

This journey isn't simply about returning to Mass or rejoining parish life. It's about coming home in the truest sense. To the Father's love, the grace of the sacraments, the habit of prayer, and the Church that, though imperfect, still holds the fullness of truth. Home is where we stop trying to earn God's love and finally begin receiving it. It's where we're known, forgiven, and welcomed, not for having it all figured out, but for coming back with honesty and humility.

This book has been about the journey back to that home. Home isn't found in the parish walls or the pew where we sit each Sunday. It's resting in something greater—the love and mercy of our Lord. A place rooted in the sacraments, where the Eucharist nourishes us, Reconciliation renews us, and prayer grounds us. Home is where we can finally breathe again, where the burden of being away lifts, and where we know we belong. We've stepped away from an old version of home, the routines that left us empty, and the habits that kept God at a distance. Now we're in a place of rediscovery, where His presence is no longer absent but right at the center.

If, by the time you're reading this chapter, you're settled into a parish, it's truly time to celebrate. Give thanks for how far God has brought you. That kind of stability, even if still imperfect, is something many people long for. But if you're still contemplating or haven't yet found your way back, those first steps still matter. Simply picking up this book is a sign that something has begun to move in you. That alone is worth honoring.

God works through small beginnings. Maybe you're showing up to Mass occasionally. Maybe you've started praying again. Or perhaps you're just beginning to ask different questions than you used to. Wherever you are, know this: He sees you. And He's already at work. Your return might not look like anyone else's, and that's okay. Faith isn't a race or a checklist. It's a relationship, and it grows little by little.

The Catholic Church is the visible sign of God's love and presence in the world. When we return, we're not met with suspicion or guilt, but with joy, and with the strength of a love that never left. Once we come home, it's a cause for celebration both here on earth and in heaven. I'm sure that Jesus and heaven itself rejoices when someone returns.

My greatest joy in returning has been the presence of Jesus in the Eucharist. In the first chapter, I shared the story of visiting my childhood church in South Carolina, the same church where I first learned about the faith. Receiving Holy Communion there again was life-changing. It brought me full circle in a way I hadn't expected. And in many ways, it was the first spark behind this book and the mission I now feel to reach other fallen-away Catholics. I hope you are also finding joy in some of your first moments back in the Church. Hold on to those moments, and don't be afraid to share them. Your story, especially the joyful parts, might be exactly what someone else needs to hear. It shows that coming back is possible for anyone, no matter how far they've wandered.

At some point in the journey back, a shift occurs. The early days are often busy, full of new habits, confessions, learning, and perhaps even marriage considerations or OCIA. We join a small group, dive back into Scripture, and begin serving at the parish. All of that matters. But there also comes a time to slow down. To stop striving and start receiving. To let yourself be still long enough to truly embrace the love of God, not just in theory, but in the steady, personal way He loves you. This kind of love isn't earned. It doesn't depend on what you've done or how much you know. It's a gift that's always been there. And now you may finally be in a place where you can receive it. That's when we begin to understand what it really means to be home.

Much of what we've discussed in this book has focused on what happens *within* the Church. But there's so much that happens outside of it, too. Our whole life changes. Priorities become clearer. Relationships grow stronger. We may feel a deeper sense of peace. We're on a mission. For me, one of the most significant changes was that I began to view everything through the lens of the Church and its teachings. What I believed became crystal clear. Coming home doesn't just change the person who attends Mass on Sundays—it changes the whole person. God calls us home so we can follow Him in everything we do, with every person we encounter.

I also hope that your view of the Church has changed, regardless of where you are on your path back. Those who left did so for many different reasons, but once we experience that reawakening, our hearts and minds begin to open. We start to see the beauty of the Church through new eyes. The Church isn't perfect, and neither are its leaders. But it's still where God meets us, where we come to worship, and where His grace is offered again and again through the sacraments.

My experience growing up Catholic left me feeling like the Church was limiting and restrictive. That was part of why I left. But coming back, I've come to see things differently. I now view the Church and its teachings as something deeply empowering. They don't confine me. They anchor me. There is absolute freedom in living as a Catholic within the Church. It brings clarity and peace I never had before. That shift has made all the difference.

As joyful as it is to look back, whether you've been home for a while or are just beginning the journey, the road doesn't stop there. It keeps unfolding, one step at a time. And part of that journey is learning how to walk with others, helping to guide them on their way home. The mission to help others find their way back belongs to us all. Following Jesus isn't only about being kind or polite. He gave His life so we could follow Him fully. And part of following Him means pointing others toward the path that led us back to Him. That may be the hardest part, but it's also the most fulfilling.

The journey home doesn't always happen all at once. For many, it unfolds slowly. That's what we'll turn to next: what it looks like when you're still on the way.

FOR THOSE STILL ON THE WAY

If you're still on the way, know that you're not forgotten, and this part is written with you in mind.

I also know that not everyone reading this is fully home yet. Some of you may still be uncertain about taking those first steps. Others may have already begun the return but carry doubts about whether it's the right thing to do, or whether it's even possible to make the Church your home again. This chapter is for you too, because God's love doesn't wait until we have arrived. His love embraces us even in the process of returning, meeting us in our uncertainty and walking with us along the way.

It's been almost ten years since I first started thinking seriously about the Catholic Church again. Occasionally, I'd visit the *Catholics Come Home* website or search online for resources about returning. I remember reading exactly what to do, step by step, but still I hesitated. During those same years, I was also trying to fit in at a local Christian church. My wife and kids went almost every Sunday, and I went from time to time, mostly for special services like Christmas or Easter. I made honest attempts, but something always felt off. It wasn't anything they were doing; it was me. I carried an awkwardness I couldn't quite explain, a sense that I didn't fully belong. Only later did I realize why. It wasn't community I was lacking; it was my Catholic faith. And it took another six years before I finally took that first step back.

That gap felt long. There were stretches of time when I didn't think about the Church at all. I still believed in God, but I wasn't drawn to the Church—until I was. Again and again, I found myself returning to memories of my Catholic faith. There was something about it I couldn't shake. At the time, I didn't realize what it was. But I missed it, more than I knew. I didn't fully understand just how much until I walked into Mass on Christmas Eve 2022. In that moment, I felt both like a stranger and like I had finally come home. It's hard to describe, but I knew deep down this was where I belonged.

That's part of why I wrote this book. I know many fallen-away Catholics carry the feeling that they won't be fully supported if they try to come back. Some believe they need to have their lives entirely in order, already free from sin, before they can even take a step toward the Church. Others simply feel lost about where to begin. I wanted this book to be different, serving as both a source of encouragement and a simple, accessible guide. Above all, I wanted to make it clear that every one of us can return, no matter how far we've wandered or how broken we feel. If you're unsure, or only beginning to take those first steps, know this: God is already reaching out to you, and His Church stands ready to welcome you home.

Many find their return unfolds slowly, and that's not unusual. You see it in my own story. The path home isn't always straightforward or quick, but I hope that the pages in this book give you greater clarity and confidence for the steps ahead, whenever they come. As I said, I carried fear about returning, and I know others do too, even if they can't put it into words. But hope is always stronger than fear. If you're still unsure of what comes next, you are not alone. Many of us have carried the same questions and hesitations.

I was recently thinking about the parable of the lost sheep in the Gospel of Matthew:

> "What do you think? If a man has a hundred sheep, and one of them has gone astray, does he not leave the ninety-nine on the hills and go in search of the one that went astray? And if he finds it, truly, I say to you, he rejoices over it more than over the ninety-nine that never went astray. So it is not the will of my Father who is in heaven that one of these little ones should perish." (Matthew 18:12–14)

I told Mary Beth not long ago that I often feel like that one lost sheep Jesus came to find. After years of drifting, he came after me, not with anger but with mercy, and carried me back on his shoulders. God never keeps score or measures distance. He is constantly pursuing all of us, especially the lost sheep. I am deeply grateful for that. But I also know I'm not the only lost sheep. Every one of us has wandered in some way, and every one of us can be that "one" he seeks out—if we open our hearts to Him. Heaven rejoices in every return. I know, because I felt that rejoicing in myself, the overwhelming relief of knowing God hadn't forgotten me.

The invitation is always there, waiting for us. Sometimes it begins with something simple: attending Mass, lighting a candle, or setting up a meeting with a priest. Other times, even that feels like too much, and the best we can do is sit quietly in the presence of God for a few moments. But grace has a way of meeting us in those small beginnings. What feels like a hesitant step today may become the very moment that changes the course of your life.

I know others have already taken those first small steps of returning. However, many still carry questions, wondering if a full return is possible or even the right thing to do. I want to reassure you that your journey isn't over. Continue to show up, move closer to the sacraments, and keep working toward full communion with the Church. No matter where you are on your journey home, even if only for a short time, you can still be an inspiration to others. Your story matters, not just for you, but for everyone.

Faith in the Catholic Church is never meant to be lived alone. It is shared in prayer, in worship, and in community. From the beginning, Jesus intended His Church to be this way. For so many years, I didn't understand that. I tried to do faith alone—just "me and Jesus." And I was lost, just like the one sheep. Returning to the Church also means celebrating a community of imperfect but faithful people. Along with the sacraments, we walk together with Christ. Coming back isn't only about reconnecting with God personally; it's also about stepping into a much bigger story and a deeper belonging.

The joy of coming home isn't just a passing feeling. It's a grace that lasts. You'll find it in the sacraments, where God meets you with mercy and gives you strength for the road ahead. You'll find it in the welcome of the Church, where faith is lived and prayers rise together. And you'll find it in the steady certainty that you are where God has called you to be. This joy doesn't fade. It deepens the more you live it, reminding you that home with God is the place you were always meant to belong. That joy has carried me every day since my return, and it still surprises me in the simplest moments of prayer and community.

And whether you've been home for some time or are still finding your way back, the same truth remains: God's love makes it possible to be fully home in his Church.

As we close, I picture us all with our eyes and hearts looking forward to what is possible only when we come home to God and walk as faithful disciples. The path is not always easy, but coming home is the greatest gift we can receive, a gift made possible only by God's grace. This invitation is not just to return, but to keep moving forward, to live your faith each day with new strength and purpose. Coming home to the Catholic Church is not the end of the story. It is the beginning of a life shaped by God's grace and lived out in His plan.

This is the moment to come home. And if you've already begun, take heart, because God himself has called you here.

Let me close this chapter with a simple prayer—for those who are home, for those still returning, and for those still unsure, wondering if it's possible.

"You have made us for Yourself, O Lord, and our heart is restless until it rests in You."
—St. Augustine, Confessions

Epilogue

BACK IN JANUARY 2025, Mary Beth was out of town on a consulting project, gone for the week. On Monday morning, I woke up with this book on my mind. I believe God spoke to me that night and inspired me to put this story into words. Initially, my intention was to write it down and possibly self-publish later. I never imagined that within a year, I would be finishing a whole book, much less signing with a publisher. Still, I sat down right away and began working on titles, outlines, and the people I hoped to reach. For the next three days, I stayed with it, shaping what would become *The Long Way Home: A Catholic Return to Faith*.

    I shared that first outline with Mary Beth and a close friend, listened to their feedback, and then spent the next nine months at my desk, writing the story of my return and how others might find their way home too.

    Writing this book has changed me, not only as a person, but as a Catholic Christian. Along the way, I've learned more about my own faith, the faith of others, and the powerful ways the Holy Spirit moves in our lives.

    What I discovered in writing this book is that this story isn't only mine—it belongs to anyone who has felt the pull of home. It was for you, the reader who longs for something more, the one who wonders if it's possible to begin again. If you've made it to this point, I hope that you see your own story reflected somewhere in mine.

    This book covers much of what a fallen-away Catholic may experience in returning to the Church: that initial pull, the reasons

Epilogue

we leave, the fears that hold us back, the sacraments that bring healing, and the hope of belonging again. In these pages, I shared moments from my childhood, my years of drifting, and my ultimate return to the faith. But this book was never just about me. At its heart is *hope*—and what is possible for all of us.

Once we return to God and His Church, we rediscover a mercy and love that have always been there, waiting for us. God's mercy, the communion of the Church, and the gift of the sacraments call us to keep growing in our relationship with Christ. This is what sustains us for a lifetime.

Thank you for taking the time to read this book. Wherever you are on your spiritual journey—whether you are already back in the Church, just taking the first steps, or still uncertain—remember that it is never too late. God does not put us on a strict timetable; He pursues each of us in His own way, and all we need to do is answer Him.

Living out our faith as Catholics today is both a challenge and a gift. God could have made the world in any way He wanted, but He gave us freedom—the freedom to choose love, to grow closer to Christ, and to love others as He loves us. And He gave us the perfect example in His Son, Jesus Christ. So continue to live your faith, stay connected to the community of His Church, and share the good news of what is possible only through Christ.

I pray that what you've read here has been helpful—whether you have already found God's light or are still searching. My greatest hope is that you find the answers you need and follow your heart back to a time when His presence was clear. That the veil might be lifted for you, as it was for me. That you may see you are loved by Jesus more than you will ever know. And that's what He wants most, for you to come home.

As I finish this book, what's on my heart most is to turn to the Lord in prayer.

> Lord Jesus, thank You for never giving up on us. You are the Good Shepherd, always seeking out the lost and calling us home. I ask You now to help all who have strayed from You and from Your Church. Help them to listen for

Your voice, to follow where You lead, and to find their way back. Give them the grace they need to walk that path with honesty and humility.

Give clarity to those who want to help others return, so that in their words and actions, Your love and mercy are seen for the truth they are. We are Your sheep, Lord. Find us, carry us, and bring us safely home.

Amen.

Appendix

Suggested Readings, Online Resources, and Prayers

FAITH IS A LIFELONG journey, and we all need companions along the way. The books, websites, and prayers listed here are ones I have found especially meaningful. I hope they can encourage and support you as you continue walking with God and His Church.

RECOMMENDED BOOKS

1. Catholic Church. *Catechism of the Catholic Church.* 2nd ed. Vatican City: Libreria Editrice Vaticana, 1997.
    The essential reference for Catholic teaching.

2. United States Conference of Catholic Bishops. *United States Catholic Catechism for Adults.* Washington, DC: United States Conference of Catholic Bishops, 2019 (revised edition).
    An accessible and comprehensive guide to Catholic teaching, written with today's faithful in mind.

Appendix

3. Barron, Robert. *Catholicism: A Journey to the Heart of the Faith*. New York: Image, 2011.
   A sweeping look at the beauty and depth of the Catholic tradition.

4. Kelly, Matthew. *Rediscover Catholicism: A Spiritual Guide to Living with Passion and Purpose*. North Palm Beach, FL: Beacon Publishing, 2010.
   An approachable invitation to see the faith with fresh eyes.

5. Fitzgerald, Maurus, ed. *Catholic Book of Prayers: Popular Catholic Prayers Arranged for Everyday Use*. New Jersey: Catholic Book Publishing Corp., 2022 (large print edition).
   A classic and widely used Catholic prayer book, offering traditional prayers and devotions for daily life.

6. Johnson, Josh, and Mike Schmitz. *Pocket Guide to the Sacrament of Reconciliation*. West Chester, PA: Ascension, 2019.
   A clear and pastoral guide to making a good confession, with practical helps and encouragement.

7. Hahn, Scott. *Understanding Our Father: Biblical Reflections on the Lord's Prayer*. Steubenville, OH: Emmaus Road Publishing, 2002.
   Scott Hahn unpacks the Lord's Prayer line by line, drawing from Scripture and the wisdom of the Church Fathers.

8. Peterson, Thomas B. *Catholics Come Home: God's Extraordinary Plan for Your Life*. New York: Image, 2013.
   An inviting book that shares stories of returning Catholics and offers encouragement for those still seeking their way home.

9. Harcourt Religion Publishers. *Catholic Prayers and Practices: A Treasury of Prayers*. Orlando, FL: Harcourt Religion Publishers, 2000.
   A collection of essential Catholic prayers, litanies, and devotions, rooted in the liturgical life of the Church.

Suggested Readings, Online Resources, and Prayers

ONLINE RESOURCES

1. United States Conference of Catholic Bishops (USCCB)—www.usccb.org. Daily readings, prayers, and Church documents.
2. Catholics Come Home—www.catholicscomehome.org. Encouragement and step-by-step guidance for those returning to the Church.
3. Formed.org—www.formed.org. Catholic films, talks, and studies (many parishes offer free access).
4. Catholic Answers—www.catholic.com. Faithful explanations of Catholic teaching, apologetics, and answers to common questions.
5. EWTN (Eternal Word Television Network)—www.ewtn.com. Catholic TV, radio, and online programming, including daily Mass and devotions.
6. Word on Fire—www.wordonfire.org. Bishop Robert Barron's ministry, offering homilies, articles, and video series on Catholic life and culture.
7. Ascension Presents—www.ascensionpress.com. Short, practical video reflections and podcasts from Catholic voices like Fr. Mike Schmitz and Fr. Josh Johnson.

ESSENTIAL PRAYERS TO RELEARN AND PRACTICE

These are some of the prayers I found most helpful when I returned. You may remember parts of them, or none at all—that's okay. What matters is beginning again. Prayer books like the *Catholic Book of Prayers* include the full texts, but here's a short guide to which ones are worth learning or revisiting:

- Sign of the Cross—the simplest prayer, and the beginning of every Catholic's journey.

Appendix

- The Our Father (Lord's Prayer)—taught to us by Jesus himself.
- Hail Mary—asking for Mary's intercession.
- Glory Be—short praise to the Trinity.
- Nicene Creed—a profession of faith prayed each Sunday and holy day at Mass.
- Apostles' Creed—the ancient baptismal creed, also prayed in the Rosary; a companion to the Nicene Creed.
- Guardian Angel Prayer—a short, comforting prayer of protection.
- St. Michael the Archangel Prayer—often said at the end of Mass for strength against temptation and evil.
- Act of Contrition—especially important when returning to confession.
- Penitential Act (I Confess. . .)—prayed at the beginning of Mass, a reminder of God's mercy.
- Hail, Holy Queen—the closing prayer of the Rosary.
- Fatima Prayer (O My Jesus. . .)—often added to each decade of the Rosary.
- Grace Before Meals—an easy way to weave prayer into daily life.

As you take your next steps, remember that these books, resources, and prayers are not meant to overwhelm you but to serve as companion resources along the way. Start small, choose what draws you, and let God guide the rest. Coming home to the Church is not the end of the journey but the beginning of a new chapter—one filled with grace, learning, and the steady presence of Christ who has been waiting for you all along.

Bibliography

While I consulted many articles, reports, and reflections in the course of writing this book, the sources listed here were especially meaningful. I did not always quote them directly, but they shaped my understanding and influenced how I approached these pages. I'm grateful for the insight they offered, and I include them here in the hope they may also be helpful to you.

Catholic Church. *Catechism of the Catholic Church.* 2nd ed. Vatican City: Libreria Editrice Vaticana, 1997.

———. *Code of Canon Law*, Book IV, Canons 998–1165. Vatican.va. Accessed July 2025. https://www.vatican.va/archive/cod-iuris-canonici/eng/documents/cic_lib4-cann998–1165_en.html#CHAPTER_IV.

Catholic News Agency. "Reconciliation on the Rise? Catholics Coming Back to Confession, Poll Suggests." *Catholic News Agency*, March 21, 2024. https://www.catholicnewsagency.com/news/259543/reconciliation-on-the-rise-catholics-coming-back-to-confession-poll-suggests.

Matysek Jr., George P. "Pew: U.S. Christianity Downturn Leveling, but Catholics Suffer Greatest Net Losses." *Catholic Review*, February 27, 2025. https://catholicreview.org/pew-u-s-christianity-downturn-leveling-but-catholics-suffer-greatest-net-losses/.

Pew Research Center. *America's Changing Religious Landscape.* Washington, DC: Pew Research Center, May 12, 2015. https://www.pewresearch.org/religion/2015/05/12/americas-changing-religious-landscape/.

———. "The Decline of Christianity in the U.S. Has Slowed, May Have Leveled Off." *Pew Research Center*, February 26, 2025. https://www.pewresearch.org/religion/2025/02/26/decline-of-christianity-in-the-us-has-slowed-may-have-leveled-off/.

Bibliography

———. *Faith in Flux: Changes in Religious Affiliation in the U.S.* Washington, DC: Pew Research Center, April 27, 2009. Revised February 2011. https://www.pewresearch.org/religion/2009/04/27/faith-in-flux3/.

Pillar Catholic. "Special Report: Why Catholics Leave." *The Pillar*, April 27, 2021. https://www.pillarcatholic.com/p/special-report-why-catholics-leave.

Pound, Marcus, and Gregory A. Ryan. "Attitudes of Catholics in England and Wales to Child Sexual Abuse in the Catholic Church." Durham University, April 2024.

United States Conference of Catholic Bishops. "Marriage and Family Life Ministries." *USCCB*. Accessed July 2025. https://www.usccb.org/topics/marriage-and-family-life-ministries/marriage-and-family.

www.ingramcontent.com/pod-product-compliance
Lightning Source LLC
Chambersburg PA
CBHW070452090426
42735CB00012B/2523